D1426578

Finding Out About
ANCIENT EGYPT

EXPLORING THE PAST SERIES

General Editor: Patrick Moore

Finding Out About

ANCIENT EGYPT

by

H. E. L. MELLERSH

Illustrated by

SALLY MELLERSH

FREDERICK MULLER LIMITED
LONDON

FIRST PUBLISHED IN GREAT BRITAIN IN 1960 BY
FREDERICK · MULLER LIMITED

PRINTED AND BOUND IN GREAT BRITAIN BY
THE GARDEN CITY PRESS LIMITED
LETCHWORTH, HERTFORDSHIRE

*Permission to reproduce photographs from the British Museum
and the Radio Times Hulton Picture Library is gratefully
acknowledged.*

CONTENTS

ILLUSTRATIONS IN THE TEXT

PHOTOGRAPHS

1

ENTER NAPOLEON

"THE MUMMY," wrote the doctor, "must first be ground to a powder, then mixed with vegetable oil till it has attained the consistency of an unguent or salve. It is then ready for use and will prove efficacious in treating breaks or sprains, inflammation, pleurisy and pneumonia." He was a mediæval doctor and he did not know any better.

Yet even if you had asked your great-great-grandfather, or *his* father if you belong to a family that has the habit of marrying young—if you could have asked him about Egypt, he would have known remarkably little, and some of what he thought he knew would probably have been wrong. It would not have been his fault: the knowledge just was not there for him to acquire it. He would have known about pyramids and mummies, though he certainly would not have ground the latter up for medicine. He would have known his Bible well, and known from that that the Egyptians were a very

ancient people living along the lower reaches of
the Nile who had been singularly unkind to
Moses and the Tribes of Israel and had got their
deserts for being so unkind. If your great-great-
grandfather had been a classical scholar—
which would have been much more likely in his
time than ours—he would have known what the
Greek historian and traveller Herodotus had
told about the Egyptians: a *very* ancient people,
with a *very* ancient priesthood, who had been
wise when the Greeks were still ignorant barba-
rians. Of what that wisdom consisted, however,
neither Herodotus nor consequently your
grandfather's grandfather had been quite so
clear.

Then there had been, much more recently,
some good books of travel. They told of the
Wonders of Egypt, always the "wonders", the
Sphinx half buried in the sand, and the same old
impenetrable pyramids, the vast pillars of ruined
temples covered with strange gloomy paintings
of men with the heads of beasts and curious
"hieroglyphics" that might be writing and then
again might not. A strange, gloomy, unlikeable,
incomprehensible, slightly frightening people,
your father's great-grandfather might have told
you; living before history really began, and best
left alone for more rewarding studies such as of
the ancient Greeks, or Euclid, or Latin grammar. "Egypt? Get on with your work, boy!"

"Egypt? Read your Bible, girl, and don't bother me!"

Fortunately, Napoleon has changed all that.

Napoleon? That may well seem a surprising name to appear at the beginning of a book on ancient Egypt. What had he to do with the place? The answer is, a very great deal. As a young man, Napoleon was fascinated by Egypt. More practically he saw it as the stepping-stone to the conquest of Britain's Indian possessions and so in the end of Great Britain herself. His imagination and his ambition both pointed the same way.

"Bourrienne," he said to his secretary one day in 1798, "I do not wish to remain here." "Here" was Paris, and Napoleon was a slim hero of twenty-eight, already the champion of revolutionary France but likely to lose favour if he did not go on being spectacular. "There is nothing to do," he continued. "They will not listen to anything. Everything wears out here. . . . Great celebrity can be won only in the East."

So East Napoleon went, with the blessing of the revolutionary government, with 38,000 seasoned troops, and—to show that he was not just a common conqueror—a wonderful squad of *savants*, illustrious mathematicians, geologists, chemists, artists and antiquarians. Egypt was going to be "opened up".

She was opened up. Or at least, a good beginning was made in the process. This too was in spite of the fact that Napoleon's campaign ended in defeat and the ignominious desertion by their leader of those 38,000 seasoned troops and the little band of experts. The troops had found little to their taste: a land of too much sun, no wine, and only brackish water, of ignorant and fanatical peasants who lived in mud hovels as they had apparently lived for centuries, and who had no greater regard for modern French civilization than to try to murder you if you so much as put your nose outside the camp. The experts did better, producing over the ensuing years sumptuous volumes called *Description de l'Egypte* which delighted and impressed the learned gentlemen of all the capitals of Europe. One other thing these antiquarians and scientists must have done—they must have impressed the troops themselves with the importance of the culture of Egypt, however much the amenities of the miserable place left everything to be desired.

This is so because one cannot readily imagine that ordinary soldiers, knocking down a fort once belonging to the enemy, would have been likely to pause for long just because they found in the wall a stone with a lot of writing and strange figures incised into it. Rather it would be "What do I do with this, corporal?" "Bust it up, of course! Get on with the job!" But perhaps it was not only the influence of the Learned Squad, whom the men nicknamed "the donkeys". Perhaps the silent, changeless, sunsoaked mystery of Egypt, the evidence everywhere of fabulous age, had somewhat affected even the most hard-bitten of Napoleon's campaigners. Anyway, the soldiers showed the stone to the lieutenant, and the lieutenant said "Keep it", and at length Napoleon heard of it; and he had copies made of it and sent to the capitals of Europe; and finally the British demanded it as part of the spoils of their victory and found a place for it in the British Museum. And there among the towering stone statues of the Pharaohs it stands to this day.

"It" is of course the Rosetta Stone, found at Rosetta on the coast of the Nile Delta. The stone, as you can see in the photograph, is covered with lines of writing, of three kinds. The top two are incomprehensible and illegible, two different sorts, presumably, of Egyptian writing; the third is familiar, at least to the classical scholar, for it is Greek. If you set up a stone with three different kinds of writing on it, you are almost certainly saying the same thing three times over: those who want to read it and cannot make out one of the scripts may be able to succeed with another.

The discovery of the Rosetta Stone caused great excitement. Napoleon's reputation went up in the estimation of the scholars if not much

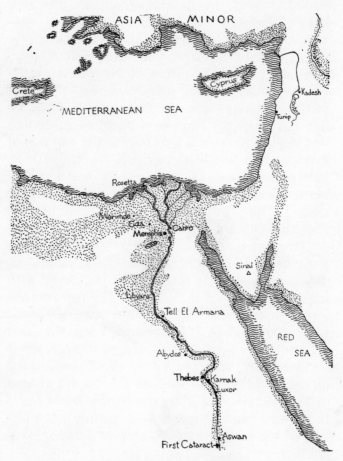

Egypt and her neighbours

at the moment with the soldiers. His whim to ship a load of "donkeys" had been justified. For here surely was the key, and one that would turn with ease, to the decipherment of the Egyptian writing; here was the chance, appearing luckily at almost the beginning of the world's serious enquiry into the ancient Egyptians' life and history, to learn, not only from the things they had left behind them but actually from their own tongues, what Egyptians had said and written about Egyptians.

People were indeed right: here was the key. But that it was an easy key to turn was horribly distant from the truth.

2

THE NOT-SO-EASY TASK

THE FIRST thing to realize about the Rosetta Stone is that the middle of the three writings is no more than another Egyptian way of putting down what is written at the top. This has been done in the Egyptians' *cursive* or "running" way of writing—our ordinary writing is a cursive form of capital lettering. The difference is that the Egyptian equivalent of our capital lettering is so much more complicated than ours that the change to a quick easy "cursive" hand produces something totally unrecognizable as having any connection with the original. To the original Egyptian writing (top of the Rosetta Stone) there has been given the Greek name *hieroglyphs*, meaning "priestly-carved" or incised (or for that matter painted) by the priests. To the cursive has been given the name *demotic* or "the common people's". As you can imagine, the second arrived a good deal later than the first. Having established this fact, we can now proceed to forget the *demotic*—which is indeed what the early decipherers would have been wise to have done, until they had mastered the hieroglyphics; though they can hardly be expected to have known that.

They, of course, knew very little. What was believed when the Rosetta Stone came to light is interesting. It had even been disputed that these strange signs which appeared everywhere on things of ancient Egypt, on massive pillars down to the winding sheets of mummies, constituted writing at all. True, there existed simple signs such as ovals and little squares and half-circles and dots and dashes; but mostly there were pictures, pictures of snakes and lions and birds and men and faces and the like. Pictures they were, then, and no more—which was an opinion less stupid than it sounds, because often the hieroglyphs appeared as no more than decorations in the corners of larger paintings, which were of course undoubtedly pictures.

But most pictures tell a story. And so does writing. Perhaps, then, pictures developed into writing?

That is of course the exact truth. What people a hundred and fifty years ago were not yet realizing was how far the ancient Egyptians had reached in the process of developing the mere picture-that-tells-a-story into true and proper writing, and how early in their history they had been so clever as to take the necessary steps. Even those who did realize that hieroglyphics constituted a proper form of writing were, at least before Napoleon's time, pretty ridiculous in the efforts they made at interpretation. We must not laugh at them—it needed a genius to do any better. For one thing, possessing the Bible stories and not a very great deal else as a source of knowledge of the Egyptians, and thinking perhaps that at least the demotic script did not look unlike Hebrew, people were always trying to make the Egyptian writing into nothing more than a translation of the Bible in general and the Book of Exodus in particular. Even more foolishly, people were convinced that the whole business was highly mysterious and terribly symbolic. A Greek-speaking Egyptian of the fifth century A.D., by name Horapollo, had put them on to this tack, and scholars had never managed to get off it. "When," had announced Horapollo, "the Egyptians wished to denote a man that passes fearlessly through the evils which assail him, even until death, they draw the skin of a hyena. For if a man clothe himself in this skin and pass through any of his enemies, he will be injured by none but pass through without fear." "When," continued Horapollo, with even less reason, "anything unlawful or hateful, they draw a fish." An earnest German professor of mathematics in the seventeenth century, still mesmerized by Horapollo, took a set of hieroglyphics which we now know spell out no more than the Roman title *Auto-crator*, and made this of it:

> *The author of fruitfulness and of all vegeta-tion is Osiris, whose productive force was produced in his kingdom out of heaven through the holy Mophta.*

Neither he nor anyone else knew who the holy Mophta was. High time, you may well say, for the Rosetta Stone!

But, as we have observed, this wonderful stroke of luck, this famous key, did not prove anywhere near so easy to manipulate successfully as people had at first assumed. Let us take a look at the stone ourselves, or rather its illustration. A few difficulties are obvious. To begin with, a good deal of the hieroglyphic script is missing; and where this is nearly complete, the equivalent Greek has lost the end of all its lines. How do you get to know where the two *fit*? How do you know even which way the hieroglyphic runs— left to right or right to left, or even first one way and then the other (which is quite a common way for early writing to go)? * Then how *close* is the translation into Greek from the Egyptian? It may only be rough. No translation of one people's and civilization's language into that of a totally dif-ferent people and civilization can ever be exact, because they have different idioms, different ways

* Actually it runs in this instance from right to left; the human and animal figures always face *into* the way of reading.

of thought—try translating a modern advertisement or newspaper heading into Latin if you know any, or as a reverse process a piece of the Authorized Version of the Bible into, say, crooner's American! And most important of all, even supposing that you have spotted an exact equivalent word in the hieroglyphics and the Greek, what do those hieroglyphic signs *represent*? Are they letters of an alphabet? And if so, what? Is each sign a combination of letters, a sound? Or do some or all of them represent ideas and not sounds at all?

Now all this has been set out certainly not to confuse the reader. It shows some of the difficulties. But it is actually intended to do something more, to introduce the idea: just how did any early people ever build up a successful way of writing "from scratch"? For only by having some understanding of how it all began is it ever possible to decipher any primitive form of writing. At the same time such an understanding, or even a glimmering of it, which is perhaps all we can hope for, will help us to realize what an achievement it must have been for the Egyptian people to learn to write.

Perhaps you had read to you as a child Rudyard Kipling's "Just So" story called *The Alphabet*—which is a good deal more informative than you probably then imagined. This tells of an imaginary little girl, Taffy, who did just this thing and invented writing, as you might say without knowing it. She was out fishing with her father, and wanted a stranger that they had met to go back with a message to her mother asking for a fishing-spear that her father had forgotten to bring. So she *drew*. She drew her father fishing. Then the spear. Then the stranger bringing it back; and so on. That the pictures did not in fact quite give the message intended, and that things consequently went rather wrong, does not matter. She had the right idea.

The palette of Narmer

So had the Egyptians the right idea. And they, as you would imagine, went further.

Here is the palette of a ruler called Narmer.*
You can see what he is doing; he is seizing another
man by the top-knot and is about, as we would
say, to "sock him one". This *symbolizes* that he
is victorious over his enemies. But who is he,
and who exactly is his captive enemy? Look
at the little things drawn on the right of the
captive's head. They represent, it is believed, a
fish-spear and a lake or pool. He comes from
such a place; he is, we may guess, named after
that place; in fact he is "Lord Fishpool".

Now something very important has happened
here: the picture stands not merely for a *thing*,
it stands for a *sound*. Here is the sounds-game
sometimes called Rebuses, the game we play
when we are presented with a picture of a weather-
cock, a part of a pig, and a barrel:

and we guess or "read" South-ham-tun or
Southampton. The possibilities, once you have
invented that idea, are endless. If only you

* Otherwise known as Menes and the founder of "Dynastic"
(explained later) Egypt. The palette was for mixing eye-paint,
made from green malachite. Pretty well every Egyptian used such
a thing, partly as ladies now use "eye shadow", but mostly as a
protection against the sunlight's glare. The best people had
artistically decorated palettes, highly personal to themselves,
as men now have signet rings.

have enough signs for things with short names, such as our *ham* and *tun* and so forth, you can string out almost any longer word you like. The ancient Egyptian language, too, lent itself to this process. For one thing, consonants were much more important than vowels in their language, so much so that they did not bother about vowels at all in their writing, so that for instance the sign for the mouth, ⌒ would read RO, RA or RE, and so, you might say, virtually the letter R.

Confusing? Up to a point, yes. But we must remember that reading was never expected to be easy; neither was writing. To write well was something like learning how to paint well—you did it with loving care and an artistic appreciation, and no doubt after a terribly long time at school. To be able to read was equally to be rather an exceptional person, and to do so, even if you were an educated Egyptian, would necessarily need some considerable thought.

Another thing: as the Egyptian way of writing gradually evolved, it seemed never to discard anything. At its best, its most modern, it had *nearly* an alphabet, made up of signs such as, ⌒ "R" above. But it also retained pure pictures for things as well: a picture of a dog-headed god meant *that* god, that of a scribe really meant a scribe, and so on. Indeed the picture-method went even further, to convey an *idea*: picture of a scribe, *writing*; picture of a pair of legs, *standing*, *walking*, *running*. In the end you really get a sort of duplication, a double guide to what was meant. To give English examples is not quite fair, but it is certainly the best way to explain. It was as if we in writing the word RUN wrote first an R and then an N, and then added a little picture of two legs, as much as to say "*to run* I'm trying to get across to you and not *rain*—or for that matter *wren*".

In other words, and to use technical language, the Egyptians had invented true writing for the reason that they had reached beyond the stage of mere *pictograms*, or signs for things, and had progressed to *phonograms*, or signs for sounds. Nevertheless they had not gone all the way to produce a proper alphabet (that is, a sign for each sole, single, indivisible sound), and they had retained much of their earlier primitive methods, partly from conservatism and partly of necessity, as a guide to make up for deficiencies. They had done the job, but it was hardly a "streamlined" job—more as if somebody making a motor-car had left in a pair of pedals underneath or a pair of shafts for the non-existent horse. . . .

Now therefore we can begin to see why the decipherers, faced with the tantalizing Rosetta Stone, did not do their job in a trice, and why the Frenchman Jean François Champollion and the Englishman Dr. Thomas Young nearly worried themselves into their graves, and quar-

relled into the bargain, before Egyptian hieroglyphics could be read. Before we turn to them,
however, one thing must be remembered—lest
in following the detective story we forget what
an important thing is being detected. This is no
petty crime that is being pieced together, nor
for that matter a big one; it is a colossally important invention, the biggest perhaps that man
ever made after he had taught himself to speak.
To speak enables men to communicate with one
another, to get across ideas from one mind to
another. Writing enables men to get across
ideas from one mind to another even when the
other mind, the receiving mind, *is not there at all
but is in another place or another time.* It enables
a king, a Pharaoh, to boast to all posterity (as he
did on the Rosetta Stone, date 196 B.C.) of his
greatness and munificence; it enables a Pharaoh
to send messages across the length of his land,
messages that will be read and obeyed because
the reader will envisage the man who sent them;
it enables a common man to enlist the help of his
gods, because writing has surely a magic power far
greater than any spoken words; it enables a poor
forsaken and widowed queen (as later we shall
see) to send a heartfelt plea not merely across the
length of a land but right beyond the sea and
mountains to a distant country where reigns an
alien king whom she believes may help her.
Writing, the invention of the Egyptians, does
all that, and rather more.

3

"JE TIENS L'AFFAIRE!"

JEAN CHAMPOLLION and Thomas Young, the two most famous decipherers, were as unlike as two patchwork quilts, but had one thing in common: they were both child wonders, infant prodigies. The French boy was teaching himself Hebrew and Arabic and Chaldean from the age of eleven, and at sixteen was being elected member of the Academy of his home town of Grenoble. The English boy had read the Bible twice before he was four years old (at least, so he said) and at six had learnt by heart, to recite to his grandfather, the whole of Goldsmith's *The Deserted Village*. The one became a schoolmaster and a professor, the other a doctor and scientist and classical scholar. Both were fascinated by languages as a more ordinary boy is fascinated by keeping pets or taking radio sets to pieces.

Jean lived and thought Egyptian from the time when at the age of eight his elder brother, expecting to go on Napoleon's famous expedition, told him all the romantic things he knew and could find out about Egypt. By the time Jean was of age he had already written a book on the country (although he had never been there) and was thoroughly immersed in an effort to decipher the hieroglyphics of the Rosetta Stone. In 1814 he wrote to the foreign secretary of the British Royal Society for better copies of certain parts of the script, the stone you will remember having been inconsiderately appropriated by the British. This foreign secretary was none other than Dr. Thomas Young.

Thomas Young was one of those people who can never leave a new subject alone, who dabble in everything difficult and, disproving the adage about a Jack of all trades being master of none, usually do better as amateurs than all the professionals. He was just over forty now, and already successful and quite famous. He turned his attention, having thus had it aroused, to the Rosetta Stone.

Though we cannot follow the careers and successes of these two men in detail, we will follow Thomas Young a little way. For curiously enough, he was at the beginning more successful than the younger Frenchman. Champollion had been at the job almost continuously for several years. But he had, as it were, packed himself too full of knowledge, and like all his predecessors he was still somewhat bedevilled by too much regard for our old friend Horapollo. Young, starting with an open mind, but a very direct, methodical and acute mind, went more straightly ahead.

Young's reasoning was something like this:

It *can't* all be pictograms! What would the Egyptians do for instance when they came to a proper name, a foreign name in particular, say the name or title of a foreign conqueror? They would *have* to use the 'rebus' idea and spell out the name by pictures of things that gave the *sounds* of the syllables of it.

Very well, then! We have got the title of a foreign conqueror here on the Rosetta Stone, Ptolemy in fact, or in Greek Ptolemaios. Further, this set of hieroglyphics on the Stone, put in a frame or what the French have called a "cartouche", *is* probably the title Ptolemy, just because it is in a frame to show its importance. Assuming so, we have, I guess:

P

T

(sometimes omitted and not essential)

OLE

MA or simple M

I

OSH or OS

Here was the first real piece of decipherment (as opposed to wild guesswork). And Thomas

Young was very nearly right: the third sign, a cowboy's lasso, was really the sound of O or U,* and the lion was simply the L sound. But of course he did not rest at that. He got his friends and his friends' friends, British consuls in Egypt and the like, to scour the land for more material, more stories or documents that would give known names. The name Berenice was found—the Egyptians wrote it BRNKS!—and then Cleopatra. These served to do two things; build up more letters, and act as a check on previous efforts.

But it was not plain sailing. Very far from it. Thomas Young, who had taken up the job so confidently, as he did all jobs, began to realize why nobody had made much progress. For instance, whereas Cleopatra should have corroborated Ptolemaios by giving the same signs for L, O, P and T, it only did so for the first three, the T being different. This was always happening, more than one sign for the same sound; here the conservative Egyptian habit of never scrapping anything was encountered again, to make things more difficult. Or the reverse would seem to happen, a sign with more than one sound.

Then there were so many signs. Both Young

* But we said the Egyptians had no signs for vowels! Better perhaps to say "no signs for real and proper vowel sounds". This one is really and originally a W. Similarly, the double feather sign in Ptolemaious is really a Y. The vulture sign is often translated as an A sound, but it was originally what we call a glottal stop—the noise a cockney makes when he leaves out a "t" in the middle of a word, "bread-and-bu'er".

and Champollion were busy building up an "alphabet". Yet an alphabet never really existed; only signs-for-sounds. When the sound was a short one it approximated to a letter of our alphabet. But you could have a sign for a sound with a consonant at each end (a little face, for instance, which gave the sound *h-r* and meant "upon"), or a sign for a two-syllable or even a three-syllable sound (for instance the little picture of the sacred scarab beetle, which gave the sign *kh-p-r*).* Then there were all the signs that were not sounds at all but which remained pure pictograms or, as we have said, acted as guides or "determinatives" as they are called.

Nor did all these constitute what was really the second serious difficulty. It was all very well to fiddle about with proper names, but where were you when you got away from these? You might know from the Rosetta Stone that, for instance, the signs for a hook, a lotus flower on its stalk, a squiggle such as you get at the end of a Swiss roll (said incredibly to be a lazy way of drawing a quail chick), and a couple of diagonal lines, gave a sound something like *shuy* and meant "a decree". But the Stone gave such an infinitesimal vocabulary; what would the letters the other way round, *yush* (if there was such a word), or in any other combination mean?

* The dashes are for the unknown vowels. Literally we do not even now know *how* some words were pronounced. That, incidentally, is largely why you get so many varieties of spellings of Egyptian names: everybody has his own pet idea on the subject.

In fact, you had to *know the language*; you had to find the meaning as well as the sound, "translate" as well as what is called "transliterate".

This was where Jean Champollion particularly came into his own. It must be remembered that the material that everyone had so far been working on, the Rosetta Stone and so forth, came from very late Egypt, and conquered Egypt at that; Champollion had got firmly fixed into his head the reasonable, but wrong, assumption that when you reached back to really ancient Egyptian writing you would *not* find signs giving sounds, but only signs acting as pictures for ideas and things. Thomas Young could by now have told him better. But though Champollion knew what Young was doing, he would not take much notice—nor for that matter ever acknowledge his debt, which was why, for a time, they quarrelled. But then one day Champollion suddenly saw the light. He had acquired some material that was truly from ancient Egypt. He sat staring at a "cartouche" that included a sign which he had reason to believe had connection with the idea "to be born"; and the word for "to be born", he had further reason to believe from his knowledge of the ancient Egyptian language, would have a root with the sound MES. Then in front of this came the sun sign, the god RA. Here it was then: Ramesses. Then the ancient words *were*, at least partly, phonetic! Champollion verified this from other words, and then in wild excitement rushed out into the street and round to his elder brother, planked down what he had done, cried *"Je tiens l'affaire!* I've done the job," and promptly fainted.

The significant fact here is what we have called Champollion's knowledge of the ancient Egyptian language. No one could have a full knowledge of that, because it was dead and forgotten. But the Egyptian Christians still used in their rituals and services "Coptic", which is a direct though rather distant descendant of the language of the ancient Egyptians, something less like it than modern English is to Chaucer's or *Piers Plowman*. From an early age, Champollion had steeped himself in Coptic, ferreting out every book he could find, visiting a Coptic priest whom he found in Paris, compiling his own grammar, writing his own notes in Coptic. (A later scholar carefully took up some of these and started editing and annotating them under the impression that they were originals!) Champollion, in fact, knew the language in the way it had to be known for his particular purpose: how it behaved, how its grammar went, how it was likely to have changed from its original and lost ancient Egyptian.

Jean Champollion now shot ahead, more than making up for lost time. He was soon reading papers before the most learned scientists and linguists in Europe, and being acclaimed as a genius. Thomas Young met him a few years later in Paris, and sensed that though his rival still seemed to believe that he owed no help from anybody, he was now sufficiently successful and secure to forgive anyone who thought otherwise. The quarrel was over, and poor Thomas Young wrote to a friend that it was all no doubt a salutory lesson to his vanity, but that it "gave him the gout and the spleen"—as we, more vulgarly, might say "the pip"—to see how Champollion had forged ahead. Young had to be content with the undoubted truth that nevertheless "it's the first step that counts", and he turned largely to other things, to problems of navigation, back to such things as optics, where his greatest success lay. In his last years, however, he returned to his earlier love and was busy compiling an Egyptian grammar. He continued up to the very last—gaining the satisfaction as he said of "never having spent an idle day in his life". So died Thomas Young, a man with a remarkable brain, remarkably used.

Of course, Champollion never got all the way in decipherment. New discoveries are still being made in interpretation, and for instance a grammar written by the great modern expert, Sir Alan Gardiner, will be found to be different from that of his predecessor of thirty years or so, Sir Wallis Budge. But Jean Champollion did make possible sound translations that nearly always were, at the least, full and accurate enough to give the sense.

He reaped his reward. Suddenly famous and popular, he at last got his always-dreamt-of trip to Egypt. It was a long and fruitful one, and it was made at his country's expense. Wildly enthusiastic, he dashed about, viewing, admiring, enthusing, and, more practically, describing and copying. In 1832, still not quite forty-two years of age, worn out by a life of intense study, mixed it must be said with passionate politics— he lived through the triumphs and fall of Napoleon—he died. He had made possible the true understanding of the land and people of ancient Egypt.

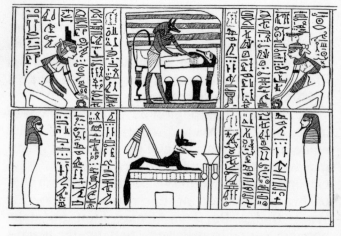

Symbols and hieroglyphics from The Book of the Dead: the goddesses Isis and Nephthys flank Anubis, the heavenly embalmer

4

EGYPT'S STORY

OF COURSE it is not true that the hieroglyphics and the deciphering of them are the only things that matter about ancient Egypt. Without them we should know a great deal less. But we should still know a great deal. A carving of the sun god sailing through the underworld tells us of an old Egyptian belief without much need for words; scenes of men harvesting or of fashionable ladies feasting tell their own story; if you study the realistic picture of the young rebel king Akhneten feasting with his family, you feel you know him as intimately as you do after reading his famous Hymn to the Sun. Champollion and Young realized this, the one starting his career with a book on the geography of ancient Egypt and the other writing an *Encyclopædia Britannica* article on every aspect of what was then known of the place. To read the hieroglyphics was not more than the most important key to the understanding of ancient Egypt.

What is surprising is that by Champollion's

time, before Napoleon's luckless invasion, the key had hardly been turned at all. Another thing is really more surprising, though we always accept it without a thought; and that is that any key should be necessary. Why should the door to a knowledge of Egypt, or for that matter to any other part of the Ancient East, ever have been shut? Here civilizations had started. Why should they not always have gone on, with their ups and downs no doubt, but yet never wholly closing, never lost and forgotten?

It is rather as if you asked your parents to tell you about their childhood, and they replied: "I really don't know; I shall have to see if I can find out." Childhoods of races and of individuals are perhaps not strictly comparable; but this fact of forgetting, of the closed book, of an almost complete shutting down, and then a conscious reopening and rediscovery is very strange. It arises from what might be called a mere "accident" of human history: the *Dark Ages* of the Western world, between the death of the Roman Empire and what all the history books call the Renaissance. The opening-up of the ancient civilizations was, you might say, the very last of the results of the Renaissance. People first had to serve their more urgent and obvious needs: give themselves, for instance, the benefits of an "industrial revolution". That done, they could turn their minds to feeding their curiosity instead of merely their bellies.

And even so this delayed action proved a slow and spasmodic affair, whether in Egypt or Mesopotamia or Crete and the Aegean or anywhere else. Throughout the nineteenth century it continued, and it still continues. But it has had always to wait upon what people considered more important things, commerce and wars and getting over the after-effects of wars. . . .

What was found by the early searchers, our Victorian forefathers and their rivals abroad, often surprised them very much. It made them revise their preconceived ideas—and like most preconceived ideas these were pretty slow in dissolving, and in fact probably have not quite done so yet. First, what they had read in the Bible and in the stories of Homer and so on was not in the slightest degree myth or just pretty fiction, but very real and largely true. Secondly, the peoples concerned were often much more important than anyone had ever realized—the Jews, and later the Greeks, having written strictly from their own point of view. Thirdly, these peoples were much more ancient than ever before imagined. And fourthly, and this applies particularly to the Egyptians, the rediscovered peoples slowly became more close and understandable, losing their aloof and sometimes even frightening and forbidding air. Certainly they were strange, and had some very strange ideas. But they were human like ourselves. And perhaps on these last two counts people were not quite so surprised as they would have been a hundred or even fifty years earlier.

One person was responsible for that: Charles Darwin, the propounder of Evolution. That the human animal was a very ancient animal, changing and evolving very, very slowly, and so with plenty of time in which to have experienced civilizations amazingly ancient and still to have been very much the same sort of creature, *that* was a new idea, and a strange one, and one which some people were very loath to believe. Nevertheless, the evidence was overwhelming, and believe it people did. All those controversies and difficulties are in the past now, and we can afford to forget them.

Yet we do benefit from the results. In the nineteenth century and after, people did do a great deal of hard thinking as well as hard searching and hard digging. We may indeed be thankful, therefore—which, of course, is not easy. We may be envious too, which is much easier. For those early archæologists—a dull name for colourful people—had a lot of excitement in the process. There was Giovanni Belzoni, for instance; he got very excited when the pyramid was in danger of falling in on his head. . . .

Before we come to him, however, we must do a little more hard thinking ourselves. This is so because we shall not easily understand what the

Egyptologists were doing and trying to do unless we know a little of the country's history ourselves —a framework, no more, on which to hang the discoveries so that they may be appreciated the better. It will be a framework that the excavators and discoverers themselves largely possessed, though very much corrected and amplified and brought up to date.

This essential framework which everybody had at his disposal was compiled by a Greek-speaking Egyptian of the third century B.C. called Manetho, and it consisted of a table of royal dynasties, just as our history books—or even, conveniently, our pencils and penknives —show a list of English kings. Manetho's was different, however, in that it covered nearly three thousand years, though he hardly knew it, and it showed no dates. The dynasties were of very unequal length (that may be expected); some were a little mythical; and some had a disconcerting habit of overlapping. Not much use, one might say—why not scrap it? Perhaps if we were beginning afresh, we would; but Egyptologists have grown up with it, and when duly expanded and corrected it is still very useful (see p. 40). The dates are mostly approximate, particularly at the beginning; but they are undoubtedly near enough never to be substantially altered. We give too, perhaps a little arbitrarily, the names of Pharaohs who are the

THE DYNASTIES OF ANCIENT EGYPT

1st and 2nd Dynasties (Narmer or Menes; Aha).	3200–2780 B.C.

OLD KINGDOM 2780–2270 B.C.
(Zoser, Cheops, Chephren, etc.)

3rd Dynasty	2780–2720 B.C.
4th Dynasty	2720–2560 B.C.
5th Dynasty	2560–2420 B.C.
6th Dynasty	2420–2270 B.C.
7th to 10th Dynasties, First Inter-mediate Period	2270–2100 B.C.

MIDDLE KINGDOM 2100–1700 B.C.
(Sesostris III, etc.)

11th Dynasty	2100–2000 B.C.
12th Dynasty	2000–1790 B.C.
13th Dynasty	1790–1700 B.C.
14th to 17th Dynasties, Second Inter-mediate Period (Hyksos)	1700–1555 B.C.

NEW EMPIRE 1555–712 B.C.
(Hatshepsut, Tuthmosis III, Amenophis II and III, Akhneten, Tutankhamen, Seti I, Ramesses II and III, etc.)

18th Dynasty	1555–1350 B.C.
19th Dynasty	1350–1200 B.C.
20th Dynasty	1200–1085 B.C.
21st to 24th Dynasties	1085– 712 B.C.

(Then follow the Late Egyptian Period, 712–525 B.C.; the Period of Persian Domination, 525–332 B.C.; the Graeco-Roman Period, 332 B.C.–A.D. 638.)

most well known and important. Manetho piled up his dynasties to the number of thirty, bringing his lists right past the Persian domination and up to the conquest by Alexander in 332 B.C.; we, however, are concerned with only genuinely ancient and autonomous Egypt.

Here is the bare, bare sketch of the story that lies behind the dynastic list. It starts further back even, very much further back than the First Dynasty.

"Once upon a time"—not a fairy-tale happening, but nevertheless a surprising one—the Sahara Desert had blossomed like a rose. Or at the least in most of its parts it had been forest or grass-land and it had supported a large number of animals and a large number of happy human hunters—we may assume they were happy because there was plenty with which to fill their bellies, and that is what matters most. Then, somewhere around 10,000 B.C., the Ice Ages, which had produced in these parts this happy state of affairs, came to an end. The result: slow, inexorable, irrevocable desiccation. In one generation you wouldn't have noticed it: just grumbled a little, got impatient when grandfather told of better hunting when he was young. But there it was. In the end—after a couple of thousand years or so—most of the animals had either disappeared altogether, or else had retreated to where there was water, to the swamps

of the Nile for instance. The obvious thing
to do was to follow them.

A less obvious thing, but a very intelligent
one and one fraught with vast significance, was
to observe that in the mud left behind by the
Nile's flooding, all plants grew with amazing
fertility, not excepting the ones that bore the
tasty and nourishing seeds that we call grain.
Then the great discovery: don't just strip an ear
of grain when you see it and pop it in your
mouth, but keep it and *plant* it. And harvest it.
With that, and with the habit of taming and
tending animals instead of just hunting them, the
great revolution had come; we call it the Neolithic Revolution, which brought mankind out of
the Old Stone Age into the New and, much
more importantly, from being only a hunter, a
mere preyer upon Nature, to being a partner
with Nature, a farmer. This did not happen only
in the Nile Valley, or even here before anywhere
else; but it did happen. Any time now, "Egypt"
could arrive.

The people who were to be Egyptians settled
in two places—the upper reaches of the Nile so
far as the river was placid, that is to the First
Cataract; and round the huge many-streamed
delta of the Nile. Learning to make and use
bronze, learning to worship differing gods and
goddesses, they learnt too to fight each other.
Finally they learnt to live in amity instead, and
to combine under one ruler and under the title of

the Two Kingdoms—a title never to be forgotten. That first ruler of a united land we have
already met, as owner of a famous palette,
Narmer or Menes. He came from the upper
kingdom and not the Delta: perhaps his high-
landers were the more warlike. His successor
was probably Aha, a strange name to our ears
for an all-powerful despot, and *his* successor
was Zoser. With Zoser begin the pyramids and
what history has called Egypt's *Old Kingdom*.
The Pharaohs must by now have been all-
powerful despots; otherwise they could never
have built the pyramids.

Now any successful despot has to learn one
thing: in order to succeed he must delegate his
authority, split up his country into departments
and put his departments under governors. This
the Pharaohs of the Old Kingdom did. Their
united country thrived; it was mostly peaceful;
and it learnt to develop the hieroglyphics in
particular and civilization in general. All good
things come to an end, however, and to delegate
has its dangers, particularly if no strong Pharaoh
is in command. There arrived weak Pharaohs
and the *First Intermediate Period*, a dull name
for what is better called a period of anarchy, a
Dark Age. It is curious, but revealing, that
Egypt should have had its Dark Ages just as
we did and indeed as did other civilizations,
including the early Greeks. Egypt had two of

them, serving us conveniently as divisions between the long settled ages of her history.

After about two hundred years of anarchy
Egypt entered into her next period of settled
rule and prosperity, the Middle Kingdom. This
is sometimes called the Middle Empire, because
there was some foreign conquest and expansion.
But the term "empire" is much best left to the
next period. There was much organized irrigation and the reclaiming of land from the desert
for fertile use; much building, and trade with the
outside world. It was still very much a feudal
age; but, rather as in English history after the
anarchy of King Stephen's reign, the local lords
found themselves a little less lordly and the
unscrupulous barons less able to be unscrupulous
with impunity. Sesostris III is the strong Pharaoh
of this period, a sort of ideal picture for Egyptians of later periods of strength and good
government, so that Pharaohs of hundreds of
years later were being called "Sesostris", just as
in Mesopotamia there was a second Sargon—
all of which tends to make ancient history very
confusing.

Then, very suddenly, came another collapse,
this time not so filled with misery perhaps but
more shattering to the Egyptians' self-esteem.
They succumbed to Asiatic invaders, and for a
century and a half were ruled by the Hyksos or
"Shepherd Kings". It was probably during this
period that Joseph and his brethren entered

Egypt—to increase and multiply and, some four hundred years later, to leave again under their leader Moses for a sojourn in the wilderness and a final settlement in Palestine.

Next we come to the New *Empire*. Perhaps the Egyptians reacted from their recent shame and defeat; perhaps changing times in the Mediterranean gave little choice to a nation between becoming warriors or becoming slaves. Whatever the reason, the Egyptians, under some efficient generals for Pharaohs, took over the invention of the horse-drawn chariot from their recent conquerors the Hyksos—perhaps you remember the magnificent plumed cavalcade of the film *The Ten Commandments*; if not, there is the picture on page 113—and proceeded to carve out for themselves an empire that reached south to Nubia and what is now the Sudan and north right up to the River Euphrates. There comes in the middle of this period not only the Jewish "Exodus", of which we have spoken, but also that extraordinary aberration, that exciting skid away from orthodoxy which is the "revolution" of the young Pharaoh Akhneten. We shall have more to tell of that. It was short-lived and a tragic failure, and the Empire was neglected in the process. There was a revival after it, but somehow rather a hectic, boastful revival, as if Egypt was consciously trying to recapture a lost greatness. Largely she never did. The dynasties tailed off towards eventual foreign conquest. That, for us, is the end of the story. As the Egyptians' unwelcome and now departed guests the Jews would have said: *Ichabod*, the Glory Has Departed. Perhaps, though, sometimes the common people were glad that it had done so, and that seed time and harvest, the welcome and prayed-for yearly inundation of the great river, still continued. . . .

5

HENCE THE PYRAMIDS

THE GREAT Sphinx and the pyramids? There they were, sticking out of the desert sand, brilliant under the blazing sun, waiting for the curious of all times to visit and inspect them, to propound wonderful theories about them, and to speculate why on earth any people should have bothered to put them up. Particularly, what was inside? People gouged holes in the lion-body of the Sphinx, no doubt while its human head up above looked down with an expression of inscrutable boredom. They attacked the pyramids with battering rams and gunpowder.

They invented wonderful theories. The greatest of these theoreticians was one Charles Piazzi Smyth, born 1819, who became no less than Astronomer Royal of Scotland. Whilst he saw in the Sphinx nothing more than sinful idolatry, he expended on the pyramids an idolatry of his own, and attributed to them every perfection and every significance. Their measurements foretold the history of the world. One three-hundred and sixtieth part of the base length of the Great Pyramid was equal to exactly one ten-millionth of half the earth's axis of rotation! Nobody seems to have had the temerity to reply to this stupendous discovery, "And so what?" Leonard Cottrell, who has broadcast and written so much about Egypt, has aptly christened these enthusiasts "the pyramidiots", and we need not worry about them further. The truth about the Egyptians is strange and significant enough without having to invent improbabilities.

The pyramids are royal tombs, neither more nor less, colossal monuments to a personage of supreme and to us unimaginable importance, as much god as king. They were built during the time of Egypt's Old Kingdom, and they are strung along the left bank of the Nile not far from the ancient Memphis or the modern Cairo. The largest, the Great Pyramid, measured 755 feet along its square base and was 481 feet in height; now, after it has crumbled more than a little, these two figures are 746 and 450. It was built by Cheops (Greek name for what was probably Kufu), who was third Pharaoh of the 3rd Dynasty. The second largest is only a little smaller, and actually appears higher because its base is higher. It was built by Cheops' successor, Chephren, who also was probably responsible for the Sphinx, which stands simply as a great guardian god to the pyramids.

The Rosetta Stone, difficult key to the Egyptian hieroglyphs. (Hieroglyphics at top, including some "cartouches"; Demotic or more cursive script second; Greek, in capitals, third.) (*Photo: British Museum.*)

Jean François Champollion, greatest of decipherers. He met, and
owed much to, Napoleon.

(*Right*) Thomas Young, English doctor, scientist and linguist—first ever to decipher with certainty an Egyptian hieroglyph.

(*Left*) Giovanni Batista Belzoni, tomb-hunter, pyramid explorer, one-time circus strong-man.

Pyramid from the air.

The two great things about the pyramids are that their builders tried to make it difficult to get into them, but that nevertheless when we Europeans came to explore them in modern times we nearly always found them robbed and empty. The thieves and scallywags of Egypt's two Dark Ages had got there before the curio-hunters and the scientists of our own times. We have long learned to get over this disappointment: one can learn a great deal from a pyramid even though its royal occupant and all his paraphernalia have been trundled out of the dark, hot, sloping passage long ago. The eighth-century Arabs, however were very disappointed. Having battered a hole in the Great Pyramid in the wrong place, they felt that luck was surely on their side when a sealing stone within was shaken loose and guided them by its resounding crash to the proper entrance. Nevertheless when they had finally penetrated they found nothing worth having—nothing, that is to say, that they could take away. Through the sixteenth, seventeenth and eighteenth centuries many European explorers followed them, and propounded varied theories as to the pyramid's use and construction; some romantic, some fantastic, some surprisingly correct. By the end of the nineteenth century and of the efforts of the great Petrie—Sir William Matthews Flinders Petrie, of whom more later—almost everything that there was to know about the

Great Pyramid and all its smaller relations was known.

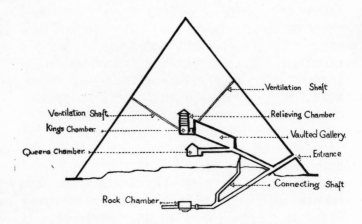

Now here is a plan of the Great Pyramid, which we shall do well to consider. If you were entering it yourself you would first make your cramped and stooping way down the narrow sloping entrance for over a hundred yards, no doubt mopping your brow more and more as you went. Then the passage would level off, and you would reach a rough unfinished chamber cut out of the living rock below the pyramid and as big as a small church, though by no means as tall. You would retrace your steps, and then two ways would be open to you, either along a narrow passage horizontally to what has been called the Queen's Chamber, though no queen ever lay buried there, or else upwards again. You would for preference be drawn upwards. For now above you opens a magnificent vaulted gallery, thirty feet high, its walls polished by the passing of the visitors of centuries. Clambering up this slope—there are no steps—you would at last enter the King's Chamber, hewn out of the solid masonry of the pyramid and lined and roofed with granite. Above you, unseen and above the flat roof of huge slabs of granite weighing in all four hundred tons, are the "relieving chambers" (the thing that looks like a pagoda in the plan) which prevent the whole vast structure caving in and crushing you to death. In one corner of the room stands the sarcophagus of the Pharaoh—empty as all before you have found it empty.

The insides of any other pyramids will be much the same: narrow passages leading to a chamber or set of chambers burrowed out of the vast solid structure, like a tiny diamond in the middle of a vast lump of coal, though not half so exciting because the diamond is hollow and the value gone.

What do the pyramids teach us?

First, they are, in spite of the impression they must inevitably give us of a lot of fuss about very little, marvellous architectural achievements. The Egyptians have already learnt to be very clever. (The semi-mythical originator of the pyramids was, by all later peoples of the Nile, known as Imhotep, and him they wellnigh worshipped as the founder of all skill and wisdom.)

Second: the pyramids are supreme engineering feats. The Great Pyramid is calculated to have been made of something like two and a third million stone slabs of two and a half tons each. Someone has calculated that with modern machines and tools it might now be built at a cost of three million pounds, but with the tools then at the Egyptians' disposal it would cost thirty million. Probably both are underestimates; but the point is the difference. The Egyptians' tools were of bronze, with some cutting edges of semiprecious stone and probably some iron sheets to protect the stone blocks whilst moving them. Their "machines" were the roller, the lever and the inclined plane. Essentially, your blocks having been floated on great rafts across the river—the quarries were unfortunately on the other side from the "holy" ground—your sole method of building upwards was to construct a sloping ramp of earth, drag your dressed stones up the slope on wooden rollers, and then lever and rock them into position with crowbars. (It is the way in which our own Stonehenge was built; but that was over a thousand years later, and was a much smaller job.) As your ramp could not become impossibly steep, it was kept at the same angle and so grew longer and longer.

The third important thing to be learnt from the pyramids is this: what tremendous and unquestioned power the Pharaohs of the old Kingdom must have had, to have been able to build them. And not only power, but prestige. Armies of workmen there must have been,

LARGE STONES RAISED BY ROCKING ON ALTERNATELY RAISED SUPPORTS

THE HIGHER THE WALL THE LONGER THE RAMP.

Block-rocking and block-raising. (C.G.=centre of gravity)

armies of what we might consider slaves. But you cannot execute so great a work without some willingness and enthusiasm. The masses of unskilled workers could have been employed only at seasons when farm work was not possible, and so they need not have felt any resentment. But beyond all that, they, and the skilled workers with them, must surely have believed that their job was a great job, a job to the glory of their King-God and so a worthy object on which to expend their strength.

Nor need that feeling have been an entirely noble and disinterested one. For if you were an ancient Egyptian, or an ancient anything-else for that matter, you would have believed that your own welfare was inescapably bound up with the prestige and glory after the death of your ruler.

That idea was part of the Egyptians' religion— of which more later. It made them build these colossal monuments: pointing up to the sky, tremendously impressive when seen glistening beneath the sun, one of the Seven Wonders of the ancient world. Only in the time of the Old Kingdom were they built, when the Pharaoh had supreme and unquestioned command over the masses of his simple people. Later Pharaohs indeed had impressive tombs, but not beneath a man-made mountain.

6

TEMPLES, TOMBS AND MUMMIES*

BUT WHAT of the hieroglyphics, you may say; where does the advantage of being able to read them come in? It comes in— with a great deal else—when you begin to explore knowledgeably the great ruins of Karnak and Luxor.

Names can be confusing, and we must get ourselves clear on this. Both Karnak and Luxor are modern names, as is of course Cairo. The *Ancient* Egyptian capital towns are in turn Memphis, near to which were built the pyramids, and Thebes. The first is at the head of the Delta, the second is some four hundred miles upstream; the first is near Cairo, the second near Karnak and Luxor. The name Thebes is itself a little confusing, because the ancient Greeks had a famous city of that name. Actually the Greeks rechristened the Egyptian town: the natives, we now know, called it No-Amun.

* A curious word, Mummy. It is from *mumuya*, Arabic for wax, one of the substances used in embalming. The extra "m" had to go in to make us pronounce it more or less correctly.

Egyptian Thebes flourished for over a thousand years, from the founding of the Middle Kingdom to the end of our story. There the great kings and their nobles built palaces to their own glory, temples to the glory of their gods, and tombs to —to what purpose? That is a difficult question, which we may be able to answer better when we have got through or round the difficulties to be met in Chapters 7 and 8. As for glory, the inscriptions which cover the obelisks* and pillars and walls of the temples redound to that of the ruler as well as of the god, if indeed not more so. This is for instance what Queen Hatshepsut (of the 19th Dynasty) had put up about her splendid monuments:

And you who after long years shall see these monuments, who shall speak of what I have done, you will say "we do not know, we do not know how they can have made a whole mountain of gold as if it were an ordinary task". . . . To gild them I have given gold by the bushel, as though it were sacks of grain. . . . When you shall hear this, do not say that is an idle boast, but "How like her this was, worthy of her father Amun".

"How like her!" might have a less complimentary meaning.

* "Cleopatra's Needle" on London's Thames Embankment is an obelisk—it is really much older than Cleopatra, being put up by Pharaoh Ramesses II, another great boaster.

However, we may allow ourselves to be impressed, as anyone who has seen these monuments has certainly been impressed. The great temple of Karnak may not be beautiful, but it is certainly colossal, overwhelming. If set down in London it would have reached from Piccadilly to Hyde Park Corner; its columns are sixty-nine feet high and nearly twelve feet thick. Champollion, seeing them, said, "They have been conceived by men a hundred feet high!"

Another colourful person who was impressed by Karnak, and at about the same time, was "Strong Man" Giovanni Battista Belzoni. From the Karnak temples he passed on to the *tombs*—and we will go with him. We shall be crossing the wide river to do so. In front of us, about a mile beyond the river, there suddenly rear up the brown, worn and fissured limestone cliffs of the Theban hills. Innumerable workmen have burrowed into them to incarcerate innumerable mummies.

It is perhaps a little unfair to dub Belzoni "strong man": he had been so much else, including an inventive engineer. He was six and a half feet tall, however, and had indeed been a strong man in a circus. In Egypt he impressed his Arab workmen by his ability to remove huge stones and occasionally to remove Arabs. He dressed as an Arab—more or less—and with his square black beard he must have looked very impressive.

He had come to Egypt to try to sell to the Sultan a method of pumping water for irrigation, and had stayed to explore the past. Having opened up the long-sealed Pyramid of Chephren, the second largest, at some considerable danger to himself, he moved up the river to do adventurous burrowings into the tombs of the Middle and New Kingdoms. He penetrated into this rather gruesome warren of tombs in the Theban hills, rightly called "The City of the Dead". He wrote a book about his adventures afterwards; and so we can tell what it would have been like to have penetrated with him amongst the mummies. Here is his description.

Of some of these tombs many persons could not withstand the suffocating air, which often causes fainting. A vast quantity of dust rises, so fine that it enters the throat and nostrils, and chokes the nose and mouth to such a degree that it requires great power of lungs to resist it and the strong effluvia of the mummies. . . . After getting through [the] passages, some of them two or three hundred yards long, you generally find a more commodious place, perhaps high enough to sit. But what a place of rest! surrounded by bodies, by heaps of mummies in all directions. . . . The blackness of the wall, the faint light given by candles or torches for want of air, the different objects that surrounded me seeming to converse with each other, and the

*Arabs with the candles or torches in their hands,
naked and covered with dust, themselves re-
sembling living mummies, absolutely formed a
scene that cannot be described.*

Signor Belzoni then does manage to describe
how he sat down—but in the wrong place, finally
landing up with mummies and cases all about
him and such a cloud of dust "as kept me motion-
less for a quarter of an hour, waiting till it
subsided again". Now this is hardly scientific
language; it is more that of a horror story. It is,
however, partly for this very reason that it has
been quoted. For it was this sort of colourful
description by colourful people that, after
Napoleon's opening, aroused the interest of the
world. That was the necessary next step, to
arouse interest; and it was certainly taken.
Everywhere there broke out ancient Egyptian
fashions, in furniture and furnishings, and
pottery, and ornaments and ways of dress. An
"Egyptian Hall" was started in London, and
there Belzoni displayed his discoveries, including
a full-scale model of a royal tomb. It was this
sort of showmanship that was going in the end to
have the desired results: public support, both in
interest and in money, for further expeditions
and excavations. Belzoni and his like went down
those long dusty passages, to where mummies lay
in serried ranks of shelves, like bales of cloth in a
warehouse, and took them out and distributed

them to the museums of the world. There began indeed a sort of international competition for the acquiring of splendid "pieces" of all sorts, the art and beauty and strangeness of ancient Egypt. Very reprehensible, no doubt, but understandable. Our own British Museum did not do so badly. . . .

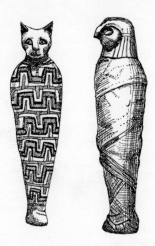

Cat and falcon. If you want your pets with you in Heaven, mummify them!

But we must leave Belzoni, shaking the dust out of his turban and beard, and become more scientific. Forget the gruesomeness and be what is called more objective! What, we must ask ourselves, does this Theban City of the Dead teach us about ancient Egypt?

First of all, we must realize that there were

three quite different kinds of tomb: the commoner's, the noble's and the Pharaoh's. It is from a description of the commoner's that we have quoted. These are communal tombs, the poor man's graveyards hollowed out of a mountainside, where to the best of his financial ability the peasant and the workman emulated his betters and did what he could to ensure a happy after-life.

The noble's effort is, as we would expect, a much more elaborate affair. Here there will be a spacious and imposing mortuary chapel, comprising at least an offertory chamber and a tomb chamber for the actual mummy-case and mummy. Around the inside of the chapel will be wall paintings. These, however, will not be religious as we understand religious. They will be more personal. There will be scenes that show the dead man's worth and importance during his life: if he is a judge we shall see him administering justice, a chief steward and we shall see him organizing a wonderful festival for his Pharaoh, a great sculptor and we shall see his workshop. Hieroglyphics will support the pictures, telling of the dead nobleman's prowess, and in no uncertain terms: "there is nothing" (to quote an instance) "of which he was ignorant in heaven, in earth, or in any part of the underworld". There will be further scenes that show what the dead man hopes for in after-life: feasting, doing the round of his estate, floating happily on the Nile, or some Elysian equivalent, with his wife and servants helping him to hunt the wild-fowl. Then at the end of the chapel will stand his statue, his own likeness, surveying the scenes, and behind it a door, a false door, into the offertory chamber where lie the meat and drink and possessions, or models thereof, which he will need in the next world. The door need only be false, for his spirit, like any ghost, will not be stopped by material walls. . . .

Lastly the kings' tombs, the final resting places of the Pharaohs. These one would expect to be even more glorious than the nobles'. Curiously enough, in one significant way, they are not. These tombs lie in the Theban mountains in a separate place, silent and remote, called the Valley of the Tombs of the Kings. That of Seti I, great warrior king of the 19th Dynasty, is typical. Here again our old friend Belzoni comes into the picture. He found the tomb robbed—as, until we get to the great discovery of 1922, all were found robbed. But he rightly considered it impressive enough to have its model shown in London (as we have said), and with an eye to the main chance he managed to sell the Pharaoh's empty sarcophagus to a wealthy Englishman for £2,000.*

Seti's tomb is colossal and magnificent. You go down steps and passages to it *470 feet* into the

* That Englishman was Sir John Soane, and the sarcophagus can still be seen in his museum in London's Lincoln's Inn Fields.

heart of the mountain. You go through pillared halls and finally to the room where the sarcophagus once stood. And everywhere, as before, there are paintings on the wall. They are symbolic and sometimes terrifying paintings of animal-headed gods and demons. We look for the scenes of happiness that are so common in the nobles' tombs: surely the Pharaoh is entitled to a life after death fuller, happier, gayer than anyone else's. But such scenes are absent—completely, gloomily, portentously absent. Why?

To answer the question, why that should be so, we need another chapter, for it is bound up with the most cherished and intimate beliefs of the Egyptians. Let us clear up another question first, however—the question of this chapter: what does the Theban City of the Dead tell us about the Egyptians?

It tells us a good deal about the dead and the way they were treated, but it really tells us more about the living. *That* is the paradox of Egyptian finds: though they mostly concern the dead, the makers of them were so keen that after-life should be depicted as like to life on earth that we know more about the living from this "dead" source, than from any other. Many of the tombs had models in them as well as pictures: the dead nobleman, for instance, sits in a little pavilion and his farm-hands march past his stock of cattle for inspection—it is the sort of thing one might build up today by careful purchase from a really good toy-shop. Often there were little individual models, most beautifully done, of the servants themselves: these were called Ushabti or *Answerers*, the idea being that they would come to the help of their dead master when called. These of course give a good idea of the ways of dress, and are sometimes revealing for the things they carry.

Cattle inspection. A tomb model

7

CLEVER PEOPLE, STRONG PEOPLE

IN TELLING the story of ancient Egypt from the point of view of how it was discovered, we can use two methods. We can either follow the course of actual discoveries, through the last century and a half or so. Or we can follow the course of ancient Egypt's own history through the couple of thousand years and more for which it lasted.

So far we have followed the first method. But now for a while we will follow the second: for this chapter we go back to the very beginnings of Egypt's story, even though much of the discovery of it is recent. Actually the discoveries of what we are going to talk about spread themselves pretty widely, and not only in time but in space too. We shall be concerned with more than Egypt's archæology—and in fact with something more than archæology.

First, however, a word about the course of Egyptian discovery. For a long time it went on in rather a desultory and, from our point of view, disappointing way. It did not change its methods.

From the 1820s, Champollion's time, until about the 1880s, the old method of "Find-the-curio-and-take-it-to-your-museum" was in vogue. That may be an unfair name for it, but it really seldom amounted to much more. A German called Lepsius, though a good Egyptologist, was particularly good, and ruthless, at getting stuff for the Berlin Museum. The Egyptians themselves took a hand at the game—one could hardly blame them!—and in Luxor a host of middlemen and dealers arose. It was even the occasional habit to destroy the less spectacular finds to help keep up the price of the others. The ugly, or the broken, or the everyday object such as the house-wife's cooking pot, one just threw away. But then, just about 1880, things changed. The Egyptians, with the help of the French, founded their own organization to protect their possessions of the past. And at the same time a very enlightened person, an Englishman whose name we have already mentioned, William Flinders Petrie, came upon the scene.

The young Petrie, being delicate, largely educated himself. If you are a Petrie, or a Thomas Young of "Ptolemaios" fame, this seems to work excellently; if not the results are doubtful—and even Petrie and Young became a little opinionated and intolerant. At sixteen Petrie knew the galleries of the British Museum as well as more ordinary people knew their tool-sheds, and was collecting ancient coins for that institution. Then

he did some archæological field work at Stonehenge: that was a sort of preliminary canter before he raced off to the Egyptian triumphs that
his father had planned for him. The next step
proved highly ironical. For William's father was
an enthusiastic "pyramidiot", and intended to
accompany his son on an expedition to augment
spectacularly the findings of that imaginative
Scottish Astronomer Royal, Charles Piazzi
Smyth. As it turned out, the son went without his
father—and did the exact opposite to what was
intended of him.

Petrie did much more than put the lunatic
pyramid theories in their place. He surveyed the
work of the Egyptologists in general and announced forthrightly: "A radical change is re-
quired in the way of doing all such things." Put
shortly, his method was to go carefully, never to
destroy, to record everything most accurately,
particularly as to when and where it had been
discovered, and finally to pay much greater attention to the *everyday* things discovered, the things
of no value to a museum but which could sometimes tell the intelligent and imaginative expert
more than a whole shelf-full of bright jewels and
amulets taken from a hundred near-identical
mummies. Petrie also understood the importance, when digging down in search of the past,
of *stratification*, that is to say of how far down in
the earth's strata you had penetrated. In this way,
and by scientific comparison of one site with

another, accurate *dating* of the past becomes possible.

William Flinders Petrie, later Sir William, was in fact one of the great founders of modern scientific archæology. And one of the first jobs he tackled in Egypt, after he had wiped the floor with poor Smyth, was to discover the earliest history, the dawn of history, of the country. This is where we begin to leave the strict chronology of discovery and range more widely. It will lead us, with luck, to some understanding of how ancient Egypt got its queer religion and beliefs.

First the more practical aspect. What Petrie and others discovered—we shall have to omit names, there is not room for them—was that the "Dynastic" Egyptians (from Menes onwards) could be successfully linked up with the Stone Age hunters and nomads of pre-desert times. More than that: it became clear that the "Neolithic Revolution", that tremendously important step of mankind's whereby he changed himself from a mere hunter to a farmer, from a preyer upon Nature to a partner with Nature, had first taken place around the great river valleys such as that of the Nile. Further, these same great valleys had done a tremendous amount in helping man to make the next big step forward, which was to settle down and found a "civilization".

Tigris-Euphrates and Indus were the other great river-bed cradles of civilization. And the Nile had an advantage over both. This was its inundations, its famous inundations which washed down and spread out as sediment the fertile soil from the snow-clad mountains of the south and which occurred with beautiful and foretellable regularity.

Now, that flooding and that regularity developed a need for two sorts of people: the clever person, and the strong ruling person. The clever person would foretell to the ordinary and ignorant common man—and he *was* pretty ignorant, poor fellow!—just when the all-important yearly flooding would occur. This was indeed very regular; and it was observed that it happened just at the time when the "dog star", the bright star we call Sirius, came over the horizon at the same time as did the sun. The clever person, who would become the priest, spent a great deal of time studying the heavens. He learnt to calculate with wonderful accuracy the length in days of the year—an entirely new calculation, this, for in earlier times everyone had been content to calculate only in months by the moon. The strong ruling person became of course the Pharaoh. And he was needed, because if you are going to achieve any sort of settled community, any sort of civilization, you must have a form of *central control*. Some of the harvest, for instance, must be kept lest there be a lean year; people must learn not to steal each other's cattle; particularly, where very existence depends on one life-giving river, people must learn how to control and make the most use of the yearly flood, building dykes and canals, and *not* being selfish in doing so.

Now the clever person comes in again. He must serve the Pharaoh: keep his granaries, keep his accounts, help settle disputes about land by drawing plans and calculating areas—become a writer and a mathematician; in fact, a "scribe", and a very important person at that.

So, in such ways, must Egyptian civilization have grown up. The archæologists, digging up sites on the fringe of the Nile valley and then within it, finding for instance slight but unmistakable signs of a straw-lined pit that had stored grain, or the marks of a sickle where standing corn had been cut—the archæologists have gradually, and by now pretty completely, told the story of Egypt's beginnings.

Now let us look at the non-material side. We have spoken of the inevitable rise of a Pharaoh; but we have not explained why he was so tremendously important, why his life should have been so precious, as well as his body after death. We have suggested that the clever person became the priest as well as the scribe; but we have not explained why this should have been so.

The best single word that explains it all is *magic*. And to understand that, we bring in another set of scientists who do not so much explore the past as make it intelligible. These are the anthropologists. Their job has been to study the primitive peoples who still exist, their habits and customs and beliefs and traditions, so that we may learn—amongst other things—how the primitive peoples of the distant past are likely to have thought and believed.

The Egyptians and magic, then. (Or any other ancient people and magic, for that matter; but we are only concerned with the Egyptians, and the Egyptians, it would be fair to say, were particularly prone to think in such terms.) The great thing to understand about magic is the paradox that to the primitive person, magic isn't "magic" at all—not as we understand it, that is to say, as something very queer and rather silly. To him it was on the contrary obvious common sense and reality, his substitute for science. Magic was the great cause of everything that happened, the great *unseen influence*. Do not despise him for this. We believe that a stone thrown will drop by reason of gravity, and if it hits and kills a bird in the process that is luck, or our skill. Primitive man believed that a spirit guided it, an influence, an influence called *mana* (or some equivalent name) which he at the time had managed to possess. Both gravity and *mana* are invisible; and he did not know any better and had merely chosen the wrong cause. . . .

To the primitive person there are spirits and influences everywhere. How else can he interpret

Nature? Nature is harsh, unpredictable. Yet it can be influenced. Possess enough *mana*, and you will influence her successfully. It is then surely the strong man, the great man, the king, who possesses *mana* supremely.

In fact, the strong man is a god—or half a god, or man-god. At the very least he is an intermediary, a link, between ordinary mortals and the gods. The *gods*, mark you, and not just one god. Every place has its god, every people its particular god, every important aspect of human life—love, marriage, birth, death—has its god.

So believed the Egyptians, and every other primitive people. Then there was death. That was the supreme, incomprehensible fact. When life left the body, that surely could not be the end. Perhaps the spirit still hovered about the body— perhaps it would go on hovering, go on existing, just so long as the body existed? . . .

So again have thought all primitive peoples. And this is where the Egyptians had a particular advantage, met a phenomenon which gave their thoughts a particular slant. Bury a corpse in the hot dry salty sand of their desert, and very often it will stay preserved.

From the digesting of that fact, it was a short step to the idea of artificially preserving the body; to embalming—at which practice the Egyptians, as everyone knows, were singularly expert. The belief grew, and remained and became fantastically elaborated, that the spirit would only lay hold on and retain an after-life if the body were preserved from disintegration.

That explains the Mummy. That, with the addition of the unseen power and influence of magic, explains the tomb pictures of the happy events of life on earth which are described in the last chapter: you have only to depict them, and with luck they will come to life in the other world. It does not, however, explain the lack of these pictures in the tombs of the Pharaohs. This explanation is simply another aspect of magic, the personal aspect. The Pharaoh possessed magical influence supremely and the influence would continue after death. *Therefore* his lot in the future life was not one of joy but of stern duty: he must join the gods in the other world and become one of them. . . .

All this has perhaps been rather hard going, but it is not easy to enter the mind of primitive man. Let us finish this chapter by looking at some of the *particular* aspects of ancient Egyptian thought and religion, as exemplified in the mass of writings and paintings that they have left behind.

Amun. Ra. Seth. Osiris. Isis. Horus. The names of the Egyptian gods* are legion; we cannot hope to explain them all. One reason for

* The first three of these have alternative spellings: Amon or Amen; Re; Set. How ancient Egyptians pronounced their words is everlastingly disputed, particularly as to those unwritten vowels.

Isis nursing Horus, flanked by Seth and Osiris

Thoth

Bes

Six of the Gods

their great number is the enormous conservatism of the Egyptians. They scrapped gods as seldom as they scrapped pictograms. And when the tribes and the little primitive cities amalgamated to form one people, then all the local gods were fitted somehow into the general religious picture, into what is called a *Pantheon*. But why so often were the gods animal-headed? That is not so easy to explain. For this one must think back into mankind's primitive hunting days. Then men knew the animals they hunted with an intimacy that is now quite unimaginable. They were also simple, ignorant and (as ever) magic-minded, and nowhere near so conscious of the *difference* between themselves and animals. The idea of interchange, therefore, of being at one time an animal, at one time a man, of being half-and-half, was easy and attractive. Then to that one must add the idea of *symbolism*.

Even we moderns live half our life with symbols—our country's flag, for instance. A symbol is something that *means* something else and something more, and very significantly at that. Horus, for instance, is shown as falcon-headed, because he was first of all the god of the Northern Kingdom, and there the falcon soars everlastingly beneath the sun (who is himself of course a god because he commands the day) and impresses you greatly with his great out-spread wings. Seth is jackal-headed, because he is god of night and death, the devourer. Ra is the sun god, and he has great pinions to symbolize the sun's rays. He is also represented by the scarab beetle; and in this, there is a complicated and subtle symbolism such as the Egyptians loved. The scarab beetle wraps up its eggs in a pellet of dung and then determinedly rolls the pellet to where she wants it—Fabre the great French naturalist has described most entertainingly how it is done. The Egyptians observed this. Here, in this egg-containing pellet, was a little round thing full of potential life, and making a journey. So did the sun make a journey, across the heavens; and the sun is full of potential life, in fact the giver of all life. So the sun god may be represented by a scarab beetle. . . .

Osiris and Isis and Horus are Egypt's great trinity of gods. They are in particular the gods of the common people; and for this reason we will reserve them for the next chapter, where we shall try to see more clearly just what the ordinary daily life of the ancient Egyptians was like.

8

LIFE IN ANCIENT EGYPT

WHAT A LOT the ancient Egyptians left behind to help us interpret their way of life! Yet it has its gaps and its limitations. There are no ruins of houses, for instance. It is the tomb, the house of the after-world which is built of stone; for the life on earth, mud-brick* would do. Then the written records, even personal letters, are often curiously *im*-personal, stilted, convention-bound: the Egyptians did not "let themselves go" easily. But still —we can hardly grumble.

Nearest to a typical ancient Egyptian life would be a life on the estate of a modern country gentleman, or a feudal nobleman's in mediæval times. Substitute, however, the mud and flat landscape of the broad Nile for the mud of the cart track and the field gate, and the constant sun for the proverbially uncertain weather of our own country. As a child you would have wandered about the estate carefree

* With straw to bind the mud, of course—except when Pharaoh, cross with the Jews, took the straw away to make the job harder!

and happy—and probably naked. The Egyptians were kind to their children. Even the heir to the throne would have done the same, the only difference being that he would have had a head shaved of all but a single lock.

The estate would have been more than merely a farm supplying its own produce; it would have been a self-contained community, with its still-house, its bakery, its carpenter's shop, its game-keeper's cottage, probably its smithy. Again this is like a feudal estate in almost any country. No "modern amenities", of course; but then it is surprising how you can do without modern amenities. In one way there would have even been a gain: not so many *things*, not so many possessions; but what there were were good, and beautiful. Everything made was likely to have been made well, and with loving care—what we should now call with naïve wonder "a crafts-man's job" or "a work of art": that pleasant state of affairs is something which a machine and industrial age tends to lose. There were plenty of servants, plenty of slaves—and no cash and probably, as such, no wages. Everyone lived on the estate and at least got enough to eat (except in the "dark" times), and one simply did not think in terms of "how much will it cost?" or "time is money".

This is not to say that things were idyllic. The common man lived in a mud hovel. But life was simple; and when life is simple, and even very hard, people seem to be happy, the Egyptians by many symptoms particularly so. We have spoken of the pictures and models left behind in the tombs; and often the artist delighted to put in a consciously human touch, the workman finding time to have a drink, or even sleeping under a tree; a couple of his children quarrelling and pulling each other's hair; the cat which has retired under the table

"Leggo my hair!"

after stealing a chicken. In good times the nobleman, the country gentleman, seems to have been a good and humane lord and master.

His own life and that of his family must have been very pleasant. Round his house (with a sun-awning on the roof) was a fruit and flower garden, and ideally it led down to the river, where was tied his boat. The great family expedition was to go hunting, or rather fowling: while the game flew up from the reeds, the master's wife and family held the master's legs firm so that he might make a better shot. Perhaps the pet dog and cat were taken on the expedition; perhaps the trained falcon. (At the end they would even have their reward of mummification, and so an after-life with their lord.)

Of course if you had been an ancient Egyptian you could have been a town dweller, and increasingly so as the centuries rolled by and life became more varied and sophisticated. You could have been a craftsman of one sort or another, or just a builder's labourer. In the early pyramid-building times that would not have been over-pleasant: you would have lived in a sort of barracks. But, as already suggested, that was hardly an all-the-year-round job; you were still for the most part a farmer and a peasant. Later no doubt you would have been a specialist, a "tradesman" in the mediæval sense of the word. Very possibly your town would have been "the City of the Dead", that part of Thebes given over, as we have seen, to the preparation and furnishing of the tombs of the wealthy and mighty. An increasing and an astonishing amount of Egypt's wealth was spent in preparing for the life and

The ruins of Karnak.

From "The Book of the Dead". Ani, the Priest, with his wife, before a table of offerings. On the left: goddesses, guardian apes, and the *ankh*, the life-sign, holding up the sun's disc.

Tomb painting. The hoped-for joys of Heaven: fowling on the river with your family in attendance. (*Photo: British Museum.*)

Two famous Pharaohs. (*Right*) Tuthmosis III, empire builder. (*Below*) Amenophis (or Amenhotep) III, "the Caesar Augustus of Egypt". (*Photo: British Museum.*)

comfort of the dead. Perhaps the very pleasant-
ness of life in the valley of the Nile made its
people all the more anxious to continue it, to
continue it in as like a manner as possible.

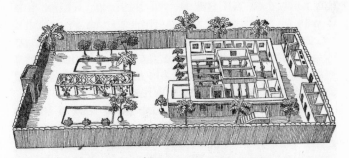

Model of nobleman's house and garden

Or you might have been a scribe or a priest.
You would have had a great deal to learn in that
case, a longer apprenticeship probably than for
any craft. There have been found "standard"
letters, in the proper form, for would-be clerks
to copy, and long portentous rituals for the
priest to learn. Even to learn to write was a major
task: not just twenty-six signs to remember, but
literally hundreds.

An enormous number of people must have
been in one way or another servants of the
Pharaoh. If you had been one of those, you
would surely have "known your place"! In the
royal kitchens the three meat-carvers had pre-
cedence over the cake-maker, who in turn
preceded the soufflé-maker and the jam-maker.

The ungrateful chief butler and the unfortunate chief baker, whose dreams you will remember Joseph interpreted,* were obviously important people. A much higher official was the Lord of the Secret of All the Royal Sayings, whose job it was to issue state invitations to the Pharaoh's presence. The Director of the King's Dress had under him such functionaries as the Valet of the Hands, the Director of Oils and Unguents, and the Keeper of the King's Wigs.

The Pharaoh himself must have had a lot to put up with. A gold necklace of a 21st Dynasty king, recently discovered, weighed no less than eleven pounds. The Pharaoh was in fact weighed down, both literally and metaphorically, with ritual and ceremony. Was he not the Sun God, or at the least his representative upon earth? His dawn and sunset, therefore, that is to say his getting up and going to bed, must be attended every day with elaborate ceremony. Why, if it were not observed, something might go wrong with the real sun on its journey! On state occasions the Pharaoh wore the particular head-dress which was symbolically appropriate, and he had tied on to his chin a little wooden beard. Of course he carried the two symbols of his power, the flail and the crook, the instrument of force and the instrument of persuasion and love respectively. . . .

* *Genesis*, Chapter 40.

The Pharaoh's wife wore a head-dress too, and a wig—and had them buried with her. By the time of the New Empire the ladies of the court were all wearing wigs, not to be symbolical but rather to be well and impressively dressed. It was "fashionable" to do so. It was also fashionable to wear lovely long pleated dresses of the most gossamer linen, and in fact to spend as long beautifying oneself with the help of one's maid as a lady of ancient Crete or pre-revolutionary France or modern Hollywood. Sophistication came to Egypt when it had acquired riches and an empire.

Royal lady of fashion

But let us return to the common people. While they would no doubt only envy the feasting, they would by no means be uninterested in all the "dressing up", or to put it more seriously the ceremonies and rituals of the Pharaoh's Court. For these were all performed essentially—and as was no doubt appreciated—for the common man's benefit, for the benefit and welfare, that

is to say, of the people and the land of Egypt.
Ceremonies have always been a part of all primitive civilizations, and Egypt was no exception:
the Pharaoh's accession for instance; the symbolic renewal from time to time of his strength;
the terrific day of his funeral. Feast days, holy
days, days of pilgrimage to the burial place of the
great god Osiris: those were the things that
relieved the monotony of life, that were the
substitute in some respects—there is nothing
sacrilegious in saying this—for the modern foot-
ball match and theatre and even "going to the
pictures". Yet of course they were something
more. They were the means by which a people—
the Egyptian or any early people—*kept together*,
developed and maintained a feeling of community and of religious purpose and comfort.

We have come back inescapably to religion;
and we must try to understand, at least a little,
what religion meant to the ancient Egyptian and
what their particular religion was about.

One could say with almost equal accuracy
that ancient Egyptian religion was:

A *pantheon* or collection of originally local gods;

or

sun worship;

or

the intimate worship of a holy family.

In practice it was a mixture of all three. For

instance: the holy family is descended from the sun god; and at the same time the purely local god, Amun of Thebes, becomes a particular manifestation of the sun and so the hyphenated "Amun-Ra". A very illogical practice, you might say. But anyone who is seeking for logic in primitive religions had better give up at once and turn to something comparatively rewarding, such as looking for a needle in a haystack!

It is the holy family that is the universal and favourite subject of worship for the Egyptians. It comprises Osiris, Isis, Horus, father and mother and son respectively. Osiris and Isis were grandchildren of Ra, the sun god, and children of Geb, the Earth, and Nut, lady of the sky. They had another brother called Seth. This is their story.

Osiris married Isis and together they ruled the world wisely and well. But Seth was jealous. He plotted to kill his brother, and eventually succeeded. He cut the body into pieces and hid them in various parts of Egypt. Isis, distraught but determined, sought and collected the pieces and with the help of the jackal-headed Anubis put them together again and brought them back to life. It was a life, however, not in this world, but the next: Osiris became the god of the dead, the judger of souls. Horus had already been born to the couple; and when he grew up he defeated the usurping Seth and won back his father's throne.

Now this story seems to us partly silly, partly gruesome. Not so to the primitive Egyptians, however. It has much in common with other *cosmogonies* or attempts to explain the universe and how things started. It runs also in line with the beliefs of all early agriculturalists, who were much impressed that the corn and all Nature had to die in the autumn in order to live again in the spring, and who observed that spilt blood can fertilize the earth. Fortunately this is too big a subject for us to tackle here. The point is that the Egyptians did much to *sublimate* this story, to spiritualize and humanize it so that the ordinary man of later and less crude times could not only accept it but also worship and draw comfort from its characters. Horus became the pattern of all dutiful and heroic sons, Isis the loving wife and mother whose patient determination is rewarded in the end. You could pray to Horus and Isis.

Osiris, the father, became, as we have said, the great Judge of Souls. There grew up a vast literature of the dead, instructions on what to say when you met the great judge, what his tests would be before you could taste the pleasures of after-life, how to pass the tests. These, written on papyrus,* have been collected by the archæologists and given the general title of *The Book of the Dead*. The scenes of the Judgment also

* Made from reed stems; hence our word *paper*.

appear always on the walls of the tomb.*
There lies behind it all the beginnings of a con-
science and a sense of sin—the realization, in
other words, that if you want to go to Heaven
you must do good upon this earth.

Unfortunately, however, we cannot credit the
Egyptians with a wholly enlightened religion.
Far from it. It was possible to pass the Great
Judge not so much by purity of living as by
enlisting the help of the other gods, by knowing
the right answers, by spells and incantations.
In other words, magic and the belief in magic
were certainly not dead. Nor, it seems, were the
Egyptians very clear in their minds about good
and evil. Seth, horribly headed with horns and
beak, was an evil god; yet he was worshipped.
In fact there were demons as well as gods, and
you were a little confused as to the difference
between them or even whether there was any
difference. So you prayed to, and propitiated,
both sorts. . . .

On that note, to give a fair and not too rosy
picture of the Egyptians and their ways of life
and of thinking, we may conveniently close the
chapter. It is the note really of fear. It is curious
how people seem to be able to live with a good
deal of fear in their lives and still on the whole
be happy. If you believe in magic you will
always be fearful—for *anything* may happen,

* There is one such set of scenes reproduced round an upstairs
Egyptian room in the British Museum.

and there are a terrible lot of evil spirits about, and people who can control evil spirits and make the worst happen! Egyptians, in fact, were essentially superstitious—and here as a tailpiece are two examples of their superstition:

1. If you are stung by a scorpion, get someone quickly to paint on your skin the necessary incantation; and then *lick it off*!

2. "Mayest thou flow away, he who comes in the darkness and enters in furtively, with his nose behind him, and his face reversed, failing in that for which he came!" *That* you will chant if you are a mother leaning over your sleeping baby and afraid lest evil spirits shall enter and harm him.

There is a cheerful side to this, of course. If you really believe in magic, your fear goes. Your babe remains safe. And as for the scorpion sting, you probably have the sense to do something practical as well—and believe, when you are cured, that the spell was as efficacious as the medicine!

9

THE UNEXPECTED TABLETS

"SURELY LIFE in Egypt can't have been the same all the time?" That might be a deserved comment on the last chapter, where we have talked nowhere of dates and rather as if to have lived in Egypt in 3000 B.C. would have been very little different from living there a couple of thousand years later—as well say that living in England now is like living when Queen Boadicea was rampaging around.

Of course things in Egypt did not always remain the same. None the less, the analogy with the present day is completely false. That is something to be realized, the comparative changelessness of ancient times. This is particularly true of Egypt: once again we must stress the congenital conservatism, the natural desire to stay put, of her people. At least from the time of the founding of the Middle Kingdom to the beginning of the break-up of the New Empire, life for the ordinary person must have been very much the same—except for the Hyksos "interlude", of course, and even then inundation and seed-time and harvest must have gone on. "Happy is the country with no history" they say; and on the whole it does seem as if Egyptians were happy.

Nevertheless, things did happen. Ancient kings have a habit of being ambitious, and Egyptian Pharaohs were not always immune from the passionate urge. It was not a New Kingdom that came after the Middle and the Old, you will remember, but a New Empire.

In the job of piecing together the history of the New Empire, the Egyptologists were given three major fillips, in the shape of finds that were in turn dramatic, unexpected and spectacular. The first occurred in 1871.

The Egyptians always had trouble with the burial of their kings. The method really possessed the seeds of its own destruction within it. For if in order to retain the dead Pharaoh's after-life and earthly influence you had not only to preserve his body but also to accompany it with all the wealthy symbolism you could think of, then you were going to so tempt robbers with the wealth—they would not trouble with the symbolism—that the tomb's chances of remaining intact were practically nil. Frightful punishments became the lot of the discovered tomb-robber. These did not deter him. In times of weak Pharaohs or bad harvests, or both, the robbers formed themselves into formidable and desperate bands—and when you come to think of it you would have to be pretty desperate to enter the awful precincts of a royal tomb, to grope your way through its forbidding passages with the painted demons and guardians flicking down on you, then to despoil the tomb, coffin and corpse of the person you believed to be a god. At the time of the 21st Dynasty, about 1000 B.C., when Egypt's greatness was really and finally disintegrating, the trouble grew so bad that the priests took a drastic and melodramatic step. They assembled the royal mummies of the New Empire—world-famous Ramesses II and his sons and forefathers—and at dead of night carried them by a narrow and difficult path into the remotest heart of the Theban mountains, there to dump them down a thirty-foot shaft into a gallery secretly prepared. At last the king's servants were successful and the robbers foiled: this secret did really remain intact, and for three thousand years.

The story of the rediscovery is yet another of thieving and intrigue. By 1871 the Egyptian Department of Antiquities had been founded to protect the dwindling national treasure. But illicit digging, stealing, dealing, still went on. A certain Ahmed Abderrasul was one of these thieves—he claimed to have been a direct descendant of the ancient tomb-robbers, so no doubt he had the urge in his blood. One day, with his brother and a stranger, he happened to stumble on the long-lost shaft and passage. Realizing that he had found something exceptional and at the same time that the stranger could not be trusted, he promptly called up: "Let me out, I've met an Afrit!"

Afrits are evil spirits. They also have a smell as evil as themselves. Ahmed accordingly returned to the place alone, killed a donkey and pushed it down the shaft to rot: undoubtedly a most evil Afrit!

In due course he removed the donkey and began to rifle the tomb. However, he dared only to sell small stuff, not the actual mummies of the Pharaohs. Even so, he was in the end a little too daring. At the head of the Department of Antiquities was one of the few Frenchmen who have been given a British knighthood, Sir Gaston Maspero. He was a great expert, and he put his knowledge to practical use: he knew that the Pharaohs of the 18th and 19th Dynasties were still lost and hidden somewhere, and he knew too that the jars and statuettes and suchlike that now kept coming on to the market belonged to those times. The tracking down proved slow and difficult. But at last it succeeded, and by means of a common turn of events too, one of the gang losing his nerve and turning informer. Maspero's assistant, in the sweltering heat of July, was taken along the mountain path and lowered into the shaft. There he was soon sitting in delighted stupefaction on the coffin of Seti I and looking across at the coffin of Ramesses II. . . .

Already the Egyptologists had read the boastings of these warrior kings of the 19th Dynasty at Karnak; now they had their mummies and such things as the parchment funerary rolls that went with them.

Next the scene shifts, to an unspectacular piece of sandy plain two hundred miles down the river from Thebes. The difficult and tortuous path of discovery was leading not so much to a better understanding of the Egyptian way of life as to a piecing together of the most historical part of Egypt's story. The years around the two centuries 1400 to 1200 B.C. were turbulent times for all the ancient world, beginning as they did with the fall of Cretan Knossos and ending with the siege of Helen's Troy. And Egypt did not lack her triumphs and troubles in those times.

The new discoveries began when in 1887 an Arab woman in the village of Tell-El-Amarna—*Tell* because here were the low *mounds* that always told of a buried city—was observed unearthing some curious tiles. She was really looking for a particular kind of deposit that could be useful to fertilize her crops, and there is a story that in her annoyance she threw some of the tiles at the inquisitive intruders who so obviously had the wrong idea. However, she consented to some of the tiles being sent to the Luxor dealers. Most arrived in powder form, but enough were left to be shown to the experts. The experts examined the markings on them— not hieroglyphics, but the cuneiform writing of Babylon—and pronounced them forgeries.

Fortunately they soon changed their mind, though not before more of the tablets had been destroyed. About three hundred and fifty were rescued, and were finally recognized for what they were: the archives of the Egyptian equivalent of our Foreign Office, dating from round about 1400 B.C.

But why here, in the middle of nowhere, why not at Thebes, or even at Memphis? Something was known of the reason, though not a tithe as much as was going to be known after Petrie had been to Amarna in 1891, a German expedition in the years before World War I, and Sir Leonard Woolley and his successor J. D. S. Pendlebury after that war. Here lay the ruins of the new capital city which the "Rebel" or "Heretic" King, Pharaoh Akhneten,* had built himself in defiance of the old ways and the old religion and the powerful priests of Amun, God of Thebes.

Here the young king had taken his lovely (and forceful) wife Nefretiti ("The Beautiful Woman Has Arrived"); here he had run up in intense haste palaces and pleasure grounds, administrative buildings, tombs: hence he had fled before his death, leaving his dream, made

* Also spelt Ikhnaton—the vowel difficulty once more.

real in stone, to crumble as inevitably if not quite so rapidly as any dream that had never materialized.

The story of these stirring times of the New Empire, as finally pieced together, will be told in the ensuing chapters. Here for the moment we are concerned only with how it was pieced together. The tablets, of course, were a great help. Being written in the Babylonian language and script, they needed to be transliterated and translated. But that by now did not present any insurmountable difficulties, an Englishman and a German—names, Rawlinson and Grotefend— having done for cuneiform what a Frenchman and an Englishman did for hieroglyphics. That these letters were so written was due to the interesting fact that Babylonian had by now become the official language of international diplomacy, just as French has been in recent times. Here was a proof, if one were needed, that Egypt was at this time a great imperial power. Actually the letters show very clearly that in the reigns of Akhneten and his father the Empire was in a very bad way and the power was for a time crumbling. Much else was learnt from the tombs discovered at Akhneten's new capital, tombs built in advance, as was the custom, for the Pharaoh's great officers of state. Here there were huge wall drawings, of the Pharaoh being kind to his favourites—again no great change in the old ways, except for the significant fact that the style of painting has become much less formal and more realistic.

But Petrie and his successors had more to do than open tombs and stare at pictures. Akhneten's brief city had become a complete and sand-covered ruin: archæology here took on the aspect with which we are now familiar, the archæology of Ur and Jericho and the like, careful digging for the walls of buildings, for odd bits of broken pottery, for significant traces rather than spectacular things. Sometimes, of

Queen Nefretiti

course, the spectacular turned up—the Germans found the famous painted limestone head of Nefretiti for instance. But more often it was patient and unspectacular hard work. Sometimes the deductions were easy and the conclusions comparatively trivial: signs of mangers and of aviaries in the palace gardens and little aquaria decorated realistically with water-lilies—a zoo then, a royal love of animals and flowers. But other signs were not so easy of interpretation. Away from the royal palace was found another palace, and it belonged apparently to Nefretiti alone. Then on some of the inscriptions her name was erased and that of one of her daughters inserted. Had the royal couple, often depicted so lovingly united, finally quarrelled? And why the daughter's name? . . .

However, we, rather than worry over the problems, will do better to hear the story, the story of the rise and fall of the Egyptian Empire. Of course this was not all disinterred at Tell-El-Amarna; there was enacted only an episode. The aftermath and the tragedy of it were made more clear to us by two further discoveries. One was the third of those listed at the beginning of this chapter. The other is an example of how archæology has become a wide and international and interlocking affair. It took place in a Turkish village in the heart of the mountains of Anatolia, with the somewhat unpronounceable name of Boghaz Keui.

10

THE TIMES OF THE REBEL KING

WITH THE advent of the New Empire
the Egyptian rulers cease to be mere
formal figureheads to us and become
real personalities. Tuthmosis (Thothmes) III looks
out at us from his statue, young, handsome,
simply but supremely self-confident. He was, in
actuality, small in stature, but as big in heart and
ambition as Napoleon—sometimes he is known
as the Napoleon of ancient Egypt.

There had been four Pharaohs of the first
Dynasty of the New Empire (the 18th) before
Tuthmosis III, four Pharaohs and then a tough
woman usurper who was both his aunt and his
stepmother* and of whom he could not be rid
until he was about thirty years of age. The young
man's grandfather had managed to extend his
conquests to the shores of the Euphrates, but the

---

* The intermarriage of the Pharaohs is notorious. It was partly
a matter of policy, partly of religion—which is curious, since all
primitive peoples abhorred such practices amongst themselves
as much as we do. But then Pharaohs were *different*. It was not
always as bad as it sounds; not often did the Pharaoh marry his
full sister.

lady, Hatshepsut, had been by no means so tough abroad as she had been at home. Tuthmosis, relieved of her, started empire building again.

He credits himself with having led seventeen separate campaigns. Mainly he was concerned with that long strip of coastal land which is the eastern end of the Mediterranean, part of which was soon to become the home of the Jews, and all of which has always been strategically important and a scene of battles. It was the passage-way between Egypt and all those peoples that by her warlike policy she was now making sometimes her vassals and always her enemies: Babylonians; Hittites; peoples whose separate entities we are only recently beginning to appreciate, Hurrians and Mitannis; a people only now beginning to be conscious of themselves as a nation, the dreaded Assyrians; and a people shadowy in the background, marauding nordic Aryans as yet known only very vaguely as "the People of the Sea". Tuthmosis fought the first, or at any rate the first recorded, battle of Megiddo (or Armageddon). He was very successful, and between campaigns enjoyed sitting back on his throne and receiving tribute in person from his vassals—his monuments at Karnak show it happening, the artist very clearly portraying the varied racial types. He built much and spectacularly.

Racial types from two wall paintings

Son of and successor to this great man is
Amenophis II. He carried on the great work
and tradition of empire. Two things are worth
recording about him. We come now to the heroic
age of Egypt: quiet peaceful people do not
naturally show up as heroic. His father was a
great archer and charioteer, but he was a greater.
On his grave he left his great bow, and on his
monuments he left his tradition: he was another
Ulysses, with a bow that no ordinary mortal
could bend. The other aspect of Amenophis II
is the reverse and ugly side of the picture. Seven
princes who had revolted he brought to Thebes
and sacrificed before the statue of Amun-Ra,
stringing up their bodies on the city wall. The

quiet peaceful ages of Egypt do not show such cruelty, even if they do not show much heroics.

Then comes Amenophis III, the magnificent, the *Roi Soleil* or the Cæsar Augustus of Egypt, but rather a lazy monarch, especially towards the end of his life: he preferred the receiving of tribute to the waging of campaigns.

We are getting close now to the time of Akhneten. Indeed Akhneten, beginning his reign under the title of Amenophis IV, is the "Magnificent's" successor and son. Some signs of restlessness and change and difficulty appear even before his father's death. For one thing an influence from the conquered countries is beginning to show: Asiatic fashions; wives and concubines imported from the Hittites and the Mitanni. Queen Tiyi, Akhneten's mother, may have been one of these; Nefretiti, his wife-to-be, another. Then for another thing, foreign religious ideas began to find favour, including *monotheism*, a worship of one god. Not a bad idea, you will say. But with Amenophis III it seems to have been little more than a cynical playing with the idea for political purposes, the purposes being to reduce the power of the priests and to give the many and varied peoples of his empire a rallying point, something to which to be loyal. Like Cæsar Augustus, this Pharaoh declared himself to be a god in his own lifetime— "Nebmare", the Great God. He also called his pleasure yacht *The Aten Gleams*. What young

Akhneten, with his poetical soul and his passionate, deadly serious worship of Aten, thought about all this is difficult to imagine.

It is not in fact very easy for us at this distance to imagine what the Aten, the new god for whom the rebel king built his new city, did mean to Akhneten—or to his subjects, which may not at all necessarily have been the same thing. The Aten was the personification of the shining disc of the sun. How then did he differ from Amun-Ra, who was at least half sun god himself? We will answer that indirectly by saying that the essential difference between the new religion and the old was that the new was monotheism as against polytheism, one god and not as before a whole regiment of gods and goddesses, administered to and boosted by an even bigger regiment of arrogant and powerful priests. Then the worship of Aten had something spiritual about it; and the Egyptians in their religion had so far been remarkably materialistic. Nor was the idea narrow or insular: Aten, the Sun, shone on the just and unjust alike, on the foreigner as well as the Egyptian. And Aten, the Sun, was beneficent, the sole and fundamental bestower of all life (which of course is quite true, for without sunlight nothing would ever have grown on this earth). The sun, therefore, and the spirit of the one true god behind it, was well fit to be worshipped. Here, to illustrate the idea, is a

translation of parts of Akhneten's very own
Hymn to the Sun:

*Thou appearest beautifully on the horizon of
    heaven,*
O living Aten the beginning of life!
When thou art risen on the eastern horizon,
Thou has filled every land with thy beauty.
*Thou art gracious, great, glistening and high over
    every land;*
*Thy rays encompass the lands to the limits of all
    that thou hast made.*
Day dawns when thou risest in the horizon,
*Thou shinest as Aten in the sky and drivest away
    darkness. . . .*
The whole earth does its work,
All cattle rest in their pastures,
The trees and herbage grow green,
The birds fly up from their nests,
Their wings are raised in praise of thy ka*
All goats jump on their feet,
*All flying and fluttering things live where thou hast
    shone upon them.*
The boats sail upstream and downstream likewise,
And all ways are open because thou hast appeared.
The fish in the river leap before thee,
Thy rays are in the midst of the sea.
*Creator of germ in woman, who makest seed in
    men,*
Who givest life to a son in his mother's womb,

* A man's spiritual double and protecting presence.

Who pacifiest him so that he may not cry,
A nurse even in the womb,
Who givest breath to vivify all that he has made.
How manifold are thy works!
They are hidden from the face of men, O sole god,
Like unto whom there is no other.

This is the work of Akhneten the poet, the idealist, the visionary. Was he then such a wonderful person, important historically? Opinions differ about that.

Opinions about him must also have differed intensely at the time. As he set off, after four years of sole rule at Thebes, to find and found his new capital; as he bent all his and all his nation's energy to building this new capital to the glory of the sole and kindly god; as he promised, as he must surely have promised, a future free from the ties of rigid rules and from the fears and superstitions of a cloud of gods—he must have seemed to many a being entirely marvellous. Like the young Wordsworth on the French Revolution, they might have cried:

> *Bliss was it in that dawn to be alive,*
> *But to be young was very heaven.*

On the other hand, to descend from the sublime to the banal, there must have been many, and many more, who regarded him as no more than "a crazy mixed-up kid", and a remarkably dangerous one at that, because he had the power to put his mad ideas into practice.

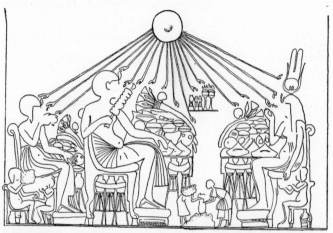

Akhneten feasting with his wife and children—the children shown small. (The sun's rays end in loving hands. Faces scratched out by later priests.)

And remember that the Egyptians were by nature a conservative-minded and tradition-loving people. The great experiment could not have lasted; and it did not. Perhaps Nefretiti, and there are signs of it, was an even greater fanatic for the new era than Akhneten himself, and a stronger-minded one at that. Perhaps Akhneten was only a well-meaning weakling. Probably his mother, the formidable Tiyi, was against him too. Certainly all the power of the priesthood and the Establishment at Thebes was against him; and they no doubt had the firmer hold on the purse-strings. Then too the purse was growing empty; you cannot expect conquered peoples and outposts of empire to go on sending in tribute if you continue to pay not the slightest attention to them. Whatever were the causes in detail, Akhneten failed—failed to do any more, that is, than leave a glorious memory behind him.

The probably true story is a sorry one of intrigue and recrimination and weakness of will. Nefretiti separated from her husband, and took with her his young half-brother, then called Tutankhaten. Akhneten, coming under the influence of his mother, took to wife (nominally but legally) one of his own young daughters and married off a second daughter to another half-brother of his called Smenkhkare.* Smenkhkare was then given equal powers as Pharaoh with Akhneten, and *returned to Thebes*. The betrayal and the capitulation had been made. Akhneten lived until he was forty-one and then died in his capital, how bitterly aware of failure no one will ever know. The half-brother and co-ruler Smenkhkare died soon afterwards. The young widow and daughter of the rebel king, changing her name from Ankhsenpa*aten* to Ankhesn*amun* ("She lives in Amun" not "in Aten"), found herself married to that other half-uncle of hers who had

---

* This sort of apparently ridiculous and unpronounceable spelling becomes more reasonable when one realizes that *kh* is a single sound or letter in Egyptian—pronounced rather like the Scottish *ch* in *loch*. With hyphens in between it is more comprehensible: Smenkh-Ka-Re (or Ra).

been spirited off by Nefretiti and who was now the heir to the throne.

In due course, and undoubtedly with due ceremony, the victorious priests and officials at Thebes crowned this frail and pathetic young king. They made him change his name too, round full circle from the change that his predecessor had made: "Living Image" not of the upstart god but of the old:

TUTANKHAMEN

11

THE BUNCH OF WILD FLOWERS

DURING THIS time of revolution and counter-revolution, Egypt must have been living, as we say, on her fat. What amazed the discoverers when they found out about it was how much fat there was to live on.

The ancient priests' shifting of Pharaohs' coffins had not been such a simple business as that single midnight super-flit we told of in Chapter 9. Some did not get moved at all. Some, in their caretakers' efforts to avoid the thieves, had been moved more than once. Thirteen were found dumped together in the tomb of a fourteenth. One who was thought to be the Pharaoh of Moses and the Jewish Exodus was missing for a long time, and people said "Of course you won't find him, he got drowned in the Red Sea!" —but then they did find him, and came to the conclusion that he was not the Exodus Pharaoh after all. So it went on, and when the nineteenth century reached its end there were still a few Pharaohs unaccounted for; opinion was divided as to whether the Valley of the Kings was worth searching any further or was completely played out.

One who believed that the valley was not played out was the son of a fashionable animal-painter who had inherited his father's skill in draughtsmanship. He got a job in the British Museum and then went digging in Egypt, learning from that best of all teachers, Flinders Petrie. His name was Howard Carter. Carter even believed, with a few other optimists, that one day the miracle might happen and a Pharaoh's tomb would be found intact and unrobbed. This was the time when rich men, attracted by the romance of Egyptian discovery, took to wintering in Luxor, now quite a fashionable resort, and interesting themselves in excavation. They usually employed experts for the job. Carter worked in this way for an American, Theodore Davis. Then an Englishman, or rather a Welshman, came upon the scene, recuperating from a motor accident. That was in 1907. He recovered his health but succumbed to the prevailing passion and bought a concession to dig. The young pupil of Petrie was recommended to him; and so began the very fruitful though not always smooth-running partnership between Lord Carnarvon and Howard Carter.

Their success in finding the tomb of Tutankhamen is well known—indeed it caused such an intense excitement at the time that the stream of visitors and press of pressmen nearly made work impossible, and caused all sorts of complications and quarrels and bad blood. It had not been until 1914 that permission to dig actually in the Valley of the Kings had been granted to Lord Carnarvon, and then the war had intervened. Resuming after it, Carter dug indefatigably and systematically each winter up to 1921. Twice without knowing it he had come within no less than two yards of the hidden entry to Tutankhamen's tomb. And it was for this tomb that Carter was now definitely searching; for not only was Tutankhamen one of the few Pharaohs still unfound, but some funerary linens of his had been found by the American excavator. As yet, however, nothing more had been discovered.

So often in archæology has the great discovery been made just when everyone concerned was about to give up in despair. The same thing happened here. In the summer of 1922 Lord Carnarvon asked Howard Carter to come for a visit to his castle. He broke the news gently that he really did not think he could afford any more funds. Carter pleaded and showed him his map of the valley. There was nowhere left to dig! suggested Carnarvon. But there was, answered Carter: this little corner intentionally left, because to dig there would have disturbed visitors to an already opened tomb. Tuthankhamen might lie there!

On the other hand he might not. Lord Carnarvon was regretfully unconvinced. "Then," said Carter, "if you'll let me use your concession I'll dig at my own expense!" Carnarvon was a sportsman and was impressed by such a sporting offer. He succumbed, and gave his blessing and his funds. Howard Carter returned to Egypt on October 28th; and nine days later he was sending this telegram to his patron:

At last you have made wonderful discovery in valley; a magnificent tomb with seals intact; re-covered same for your arrival. Congratulations.

When Carnarvon arrived—with Sir Alan Gardiner, the greatest living expert on hieroglyphics—and when the stairway down to the entrance had been again unblocked, both a thrill and a disappointment met the little group. Firstly, this was without question Tutankhamen's tomb, for there to see was his cartouche on the seal of the door. But another and later seal accompanied it, the seal of the guardian priests. The tomb was *not* untouched. However, if the priests had thought the tomb worth resealing, then presumably any robbery that there had been was not a total one.

With that rather doubtful comfort, Carter set to work. He proved to be right. There had been a robbery. But the thieves had been disturbed, and though they had jumbled things together and left chaos behind them—they had run off just like any modern burglar when he hears the police or the owner's key in the latch—they had surely not managed to take much with them. This conclusion was pretty certainly correct, because what they had left behind was—fabulous.

Again we cannot follow the full course of this discovery. It was long drawn out because Carter was a meticulous archæologist; nevertheless it had its moments of highly dramatic discovery as the fastnesses were in turn penetrated. There was in turn an antechamber, the burial chamber and a further room; no less than four shrines; and finally three coffins, each inside the other like a Chinese toy. The antechamber was packed with Pharaoh's paraphernalia for the next world. "We saw," said one of the first to enter, "an incredible vision, an impossible scene from a fairy-tale, an enchanted property room from an opera house of some composer's dreams." On the floor, in queer egg-shaped containers, was the Pharaoh's food—duck included. Against the wall was his chariot. In a corner lay a chair or throne, gilded and carved most beautifully with something of the realism of the artists of Akhneten: the young king is having his shoulder anointed by Ankhesnamun, his queen.

Ramesses II or "Ozymandias, King of Kings"; fighter and boaster. (*Photo: British Museum.*)

Portrait (true likeness?) of Akhneten, "the Rebel King".

Tutankhamen, the boy pharaoh: golden mummy-effigy, showing royal regalia, false beard included.

Battle picture from the walls of Karnak—reign of Seti I. Egyptians shown big, enemies little.

Everywhere there is the most superb workman-
ship.

Tutankhamen in his chariot: a highly successful hunt

As we progress towards the centre of it all,
mere gilding changes to gold. The innermost
coffin is of solid gold, and it weighed twenty stone.
It is inlaid with cornelian and lapis lazuli;
it shows beautiful enfolding eagle's wings; it is
covered with symbolisms and hieroglyphs and a
portrait head of the king. Within, in shining gold,
is a mask, another portrait more intimate still.
Those who discovered it all were not only thrilled
but awed. The funeral rites of this young dead
king—only about eighteen years old by the
evidence—were overwhelming but also somehow
pathetic. Those who penetrated after a lapse of
three and a half thousand years had a feeling of
unwarranted intrusion into things too intimate
to be disturbed. Sir Alan Gardiner tells of a

little fan of ostrich feathers that was found.
"These feathers were perfect, fluffing out just
as if they had recently been plucked. Those
feathers completely annihilated the centuries
for me. It was just as if the King had been buried
a few days before."* And something even more
appealing: amidst all this elaborate and costly
finery there lay at the entrance a little withered
bunch of wild flowers. It is not mere sentiment-
ality to imagine that Ankhesnamun dropped it
there as a final gesture of farewell.

The Egyptians were indeed very human—
though it hardly needed an opened Pharaoh's
grave to tell us that.

Now what essentially did Tutankhamen's
tomb tell the Egyptologists? In plain fact, not a
very great deal; there was for instance very little
in the way of hieroglyphics for Sir Alan Gardiner
to study; there was nothing startlingly new. But
there was certainly something to learn in a more
general way. Here was an unimportant Pharaoh,
a poor sickly youth who had reigned only a few
inglorious years and when his country's fortunes
and prestige were at a low ebb. Yet his funeral
must have been truly magnificent, and the wealth
buried with him was immense.

Did they always do this? Perhaps so: to the
ancient Egyptians, obviously, no Pharaoh was
unimportant. But possibly this was a special

* Quoted in Leonard Cottrell's *The Lost Pharaohs*.

effort on the part of the priests. The Pharaohs had come back to Thebes; the dreadful aberration of Akhneten was over. All was as before— only more so!

One thing for certain at any rate. Even at this low ebb of empire, Egypt was still immensely rich.

12

LETTERS

THE RICHES of Egypt at the centre did not help the Empire at its periphery. On the edges the cold winds of adversity blew. Or greedy eyes looked inwards.

That is what those baked clay tablets of Tell-El-Amarna have told us. They begin, you may remember, in the time of Akhneten's father, Amenophis III, the Magnificent. Then it is the vassals and allies making carefully worded demands:

> *Send me a great deal of gold! If, during the harvest, you send the gold concerning which I wrote you, then I will give you my daughter.*

That is from the King of Babylon. Perhaps Amenophis had enough wives already and did not want this king's daughter; possibly at any rate he did not want any more foreign wives, for he had the redoubtable Tiyi, together with a couple of Mitannian princesses in his harem. The brother of these princesses, Tushratta, also wrote, as follows:

You always maintained a very, very close friendship with my father. Now that we are friends, the friendship is ten times greater than with my father. Now therefore I say further to my brother: may my brother grant me ten times as much gold as to my father. Let my brother send me very much gold, immeasurably much gold; let my brother send me more gold than he did to my father.

He followed this up with:

Send me much gold, more gold! For in my brother's land gold is as common as dust.

"May Amun protect me from such a brother as this!" Amenophis must have thought. It is the letter of the typical scrounger: "It's nothing to you, you won't miss it!" This particular kinglet may, however, have felt that he had earned some reward, for he had for a while held the powerful Hittites at bay. His god, he informs Amenophis:

. . . gave my enemy into my hand, and I routed him. There was none among them that returned to his own land.

Pharaohs were not the only ancient rulers given to boasting!

But then, even in the time of Amenophis III, who had the means though he was apparently too lazy to use them, the messages begin to grow more urgent. This is from a native governor:

Oh my Lord, if the trouble of this land lies upon the heart of my Lord, let my Lord send troops, and let them come!

Not gold now, but soldiers.

With the accession of Akhneten, matters naturally grow worse: the enemies on the outskirts were not likely to remain ignorant that the new Pharaoh was a dreamer only interested in things of the spirit. It is the vital coastal strip at the eastern end of the Mediterranean that matters. The Habiru (? the Hebrews) attack from the east, the Hittites—they are the real menace—from the north. A certain Aziru the Amorite is the villain of the piece, an ancient Quisling, working against Egypt from within. "My Lord, Tunip, thy servant, speaks," reads one letter. Tunip is a fortress on the coast and it is its Egyptian governor who writes calling himself by the name of his governorship. He continues:

Who formerly could have plundered Tunip without being plundered by Menkheperre?

That is another name for Tuthmosis III, an appeal in fact to Akhneten's dynastic pride, or feeling of shame.

Now, however, we belong no more to our Lord, the King of Egypt. If his soldiers and chariots come too late, then the King of Egypt will mourn over these things which Aziru has done. . . . And now Tunip, thy city, weeps, and her tears are flowing, and there is no help for us. For twenty years we have been sending to our Lord the King, the King of Egypt, but there has not come to us a word, no not one.

A heartfelt and bitter complaint. And twenty years is a long time. Then another governor of another coast town takes up the sad tale:

Behold Aziru has fought my chiefs, and the chiefs that despatched to the city Simyra he has caused to be seized in the city. . . .

Grievous it is to say what he has done, the dog Aziru. Behold what has befallen the lands of the King on account of him; and he cried peace unto the land, and now behold what has befallen the city of Simyra—a station of my Lord, a fortress . . . and they spoil our fortress . . . ah, the cries of the place . . . a violent man (he is) and a dog!

Then a final appeal and a cry of despair:

March against him to smite him! . . . The land is the King's land; and since I have talked thus and you have not moved the city of Simyra has been lost. There is no money to buy horses; all is finished; we have been spoiled. . . . Give me thirty companies of horse with chariots, men, men . . . there is none of this for me . . . not a horse!

Surely that should have moved even Akhneten.

But perhaps he never saw these letters. Perhaps he arranged *not* to see them. Or perhaps his Foreign Minister, by name Tutu, kept them from him, being in league with Aziru—there is a letter which suggests as much.

Egypt, nevertheless, is immensely strong. Not for centuries yet will there be invasion of her land; only the outposts are crumbling. The short years roll by; and Akhneten is estranged from his wife and marries again, and dies, and the child-widow marries the new king, poor Tutankhamen, and he dies and is buried and has the little bunch of flowers thrown into his sepulchre, and the double widow is left alone. . . .

There come now letters even more dramatic in their content, and very surprising. They are from this widow, now called Ankhesnamun, and they turn up, as we said, in the little Turkish village of Boghaz Keui, where once lay the capital of the then growing Hittite Empire. They are addressed to a king of the Hittites with the rather beautiful name of Suppiluliumas.* The first one reads:

> *My husband has died, and not one son do I have. But of you it is said that you have many sons. If you will give me a son of yours, he could be my husband. For how may I take one*

* Other titles of his may be translated as "His Sunship", "The Hero" and "The Favourite of the Weather God"!

of my slaves and make him a husband and honour him?

This letter not only surprises us, it surprised Suppiluliumas. The Hittites were indeed an up-and-coming people. But to be so approached by the Queen Mother of Egypt! The King consulted his councillors—this we know from a description of the episode which was dug up with the letters. He commanded: "Go, and bring back to me reliable tidings. Perhaps they wish only to deride me; perhaps they already have a successor to the throne. Well, bring back to me reliable tidings!"

They obeyed Suppiluliumas. But he had done the wrong thing. In due course he received another letter:

Why have you spoken these words: "They wish only to deride me"? I have not written to any other country. To you alone have I written. It is said that you have many sons. Give me a son of yours; he shall be my husband and king over Egypt!

One does not disobey a second time. King Suppiluliumas sent a son. But that unlucky son never reached Thebes or the royal widow's side. He was, presumably, murdered on the way.

Such is the sad story of Queen Ankhesnamun, pieced together from two sets of evidence a thousand miles apart. She was forced to marry a third time—she was still only about twenty-four years of age—and it was probably this third husband who saw to it that the Hittite prince disappeared.

The third husband was Ay, originally one of Akhneten's chief officers, who now became Pharaoh. His reign was short and inglorious, and with him ends miserably the 18th Dynasty which had so magnificently set up an empire.

There is not, however, an end to greatness yet. The fortunes of Egypt in her time of Empire began slowly to mend. Horemhab followed Ay, and he was a fighting man, a general. He chose as successor a fellow general, an elderly man whose titles included Chief of the Archers and Vizier. He did not last long, but he continued a policy of, as we might say, mending the dykes; the southern borders, at least, he secured. He was Ramesses I—a famous name and one, you will remember, that Champollion was so thrilled to decipher.

There followed Seti I, and with him the Empire really regained much that it had lost. He campaigned in Palestine and Syria and drove back the Hittites and the lesser peoples that clustered around them. He built much at Karnak, and created for himself a magnificent tomb— the one from which Belzoni filched the sarcophagus.

Then came Seti's son Ramesses II. This is the famous Ramesses. The early Egyptologists called him the Great, ranking him in estimation with such as Tuthmosis III: he had left so many monuments, and emblazoned so many panegyrics of his victories, that they could hardly do anything else. In the next chapter we shall close this more detailed look into the most spectacular part of ancient Egypt's history, by a somewhat critical stare at Ramesses II—and his famous battle.

13

THE BATTLE OF KADESH

I met a traveller from an antique land
Who said: Two vast and trunkless legs of stone
Stand in the desert. Near them on the sand
Half sunk, a shatter'd visage lies, whose frown
And wrinkled lip and sneer of cold command
Tell that its sculptor well those passions read
Which yet survive, stamp'd on those lifeless things,
The hand that mock'd them and the heart that fed;
And on the pedestal these words appear:
"My name is Ozymandias, king of kings:
Look on my works, ye Mighty, and despair!"
Nothing beside remains. Round the decay
Of that colossal wreck, boundless and bare,
The lone and level sands stretch far away.

SHELLEY'S OZYMANDIAS is Ramesses II (a Greek version of one other of the Pharaoh's titles). And the sonnet is a fit comment with which to begin the chapter.

Ramesses' father, Seti I, boldly taking a risk and dividing his forces into three armies—Army

of Amun, Army of Seth, Army of Ra—had
inflicted on the Hittites, and their friends the
Amorites and the rest, a considerable defeat.
There had ensued an uneasy truce, with the
Hittite influence still reaching nevertheless down
into the north of Syria. The great Suppiluliumas
was dead these thirty years, but his grandson
Muwatallis was as strong and as determined and
as crafty. He collected his allies, as many as
twenty of them; and kept his fighting chariots in
trim, very good chariots; and waited. He waited,
somewhere about the 35th parallel of latitude on
the higher reaches of the Orontes, that great
south-flowing river which debouches into the
Mediterranean below the ancient Antioch and
where the long finger of Cyprus points across to
the coast. Muwatallis did not have to wait so
very long. By our way of dating, the fourteenth
century B.C. had just turned into the thirteenth;
and by the Egyptian way it was the fourth year of
Pharaoh Ramesses II. Ramesses collected his
forces, went one better than his father by having
an Army of Ptah (equivalent of the Roman
Vulcan) as well as of Ra and Amun and Seth,
and set out on the long march to meet his foe.
In the heat of late May he at length encamped
with his army of about 20,000 above the town of
Kadesh (near the present Homs). He could see
no sign of the enemy. . . .

We know more about this battle of thirty-
two and a half centuries ago than many a battle

of much later date. Ramesses had it written about *ad nauseam* (which is Latin for "until you are sick of it"); and during the last fifty years or so the long-forgotten, indeed the long-unsuspected, greatness and history of the Hittites has been disinterred and deciphered. As one would suspect, knowing the joy in boasting that filled the ancients in general and Ramesses II in particular, the two accounts do not exactly agree. But with luck and a little common sense we can arrive pretty nearly at the truth, which after all is likely to be somewhere in the middle.

Ramesses seems to have been a brave but blundering commander, Muwatallis a crafty one. Hidden behind Kadesh, the Hittite king sent spies into the enemy camp. These, disguised as peasants, allowed themselves to be captured; and told their tale. The army of Muwatallis, they said, terrified at the great Pharaoh, had retreated. Ramesses, convinced of his own greatness, seems to have believed them. Leading the Army of Amun, with Ra in support, and Seth and Ptah well in the rear, he advanced boldly. Before long the men of the Army of Ra saw the dreaded, fast, two-warrior chariots of the Hittites charging down on them from the rear. They broke and fled, rushing in confusion into the Army of Amun, which with the Pharaoh was resting and encamped. The panic spread.

Three things now saved the Egyptians from

defeat. One was the timely arrival of reinforce-
ments—nobody knows quite from where they
came, for the Armies of Seth and Ptah had been
foolishly left miles in the rear. The second was
the personal valour of Ramesses. The third was

The Egyptian camp taken by surprise—confusion on the
left

an event as familiar in the annals of battle as
are the tales of cunning spies and of surprise
attack from the rear; it even happened in the
German attack of 1918 in our own World War I.
It was this: the attackers, insufficiently dis-
ciplined or else already hungry, thirsty and
weary of battle, succumbed to the evidence in
the Egyptian camp of riches. Instead of con-
tinuing the attack ruthlessly, they stopped to loot.

The Egyptians rallied. Fighting with desperation and valour, they turned the tables on the Hittites, hurling many into the river. When night fell each combatant, claiming the victory, withdrew.

In other words, the battle of Kadesh was a draw.

You would not think so, however, if you were to read the Egyptian accounts. Some unknown and forgotten poet, a sort of incipient Eastern Homer, wrote a long saga about it. If it does not tell the strict truth it tells us something about the Egyptians and a good deal about Ramesses; we will therefore quote from it.

A good beginning is where Ramesses is surprised in his camp by the panic retreat of the Ra army.

His Majesty stepped forth like his father Month,* after he had taken up his battle dress and laid on his armour. The great team of horses that carried his Majesty was called "Victory in Thebes" and came from the great stable of Ramesses. His Majesty drove rapidly forward, thrusting into the enemy army. He was all alone and no man was with him.

The heroic touch. In just about a hundred years' time another deadly chariot, Achilles',

---

* Or Montu, his heavenly father, the war god, "the Mighty Bull". These quotations are taken from C. W. Ceram's book on the Hittites, *Narrow Pass, Black Mountain*.

will be encircling the walls of Troy; and we shall know the names of his horses too, Balius and Xanthus "of the glancing feet". Ramesses' chariots carried only one warrior; and he seems to have left even his driver behind.

Now the poem breaks into a sort of lament by the King, or you might call it a complaint, and a prayer to his God.

> "*No prince is beside me and no chariot-driver, no officer of the infantry and none of the charioteers. My foot-soldiers and my charioteers have abandoned me to the enemy, and none of them held fast to fight against him.*
>
> "*What is this now, my Father Amun? Has a father already forgotten his son? Have I ever done anything without you? Whatever I did or did not do, was it not after your saying. . . . What are these Asiatics to you, Amun? These wretches who know nothing of God? Have I not made very many monuments for you? And filled your temple with prisoners? . . . I call to you, my Father Amun. I am in the midst of strangers whom I do not know.*"

There is a nobility about that prayer, even though a certain amount of oriental bargaining. It is answered. The Pharaoh continues:

> "*I have found my heart again; my heart bursts with joy; whatever I will is done. I am*

like Month; I let fly my arrows to the right and fight to the left. . . . Behold, 2,500 chariots surround me, and now they lie hacked to pieces before my steeds. Not one of the foe could lift his hand to fight. . . . I make them fall into the water like crocodiles. They crash into one another and I go among them killing at will. . . . I killed them wherever they were, and one called to the other: 'This is no man who is among us; this is Sutekh the Mighty; Baal is in his limbs. His deeds are not the deeds of a man. Never before has one man alone, without foot-soldiers and chariots, defeated hundreds of thousands. . . .'"

Never indeed! Ramesses in the poem then seeks to rally his men:

"Take heart, take heart, my soldiers! You see my victory, though I am alone. But Amun is my protector and his hand is with me."

There is a Biblical echo here, or rather the Bible language is sometimes an echo of this Egyptian poet. But then:

"How craven you are, my chariot fighters! . . . There is not one among you to whom I have not been a benefactor in my land. Did I not stand as your master, and you were humble folk. . . . I gave to the son the possessions of his father. . . .

I lightened your taxes and I replaced for you what had been taken from you. . . . But behold, all of you together have done wretchedly, no one of you is holding firm and extending a hand to aid me as I fight. . . . As truly as the ka *of my Father Amun endures, if only I were in Egypt like my fathers who never saw the Syrians! . . ."*

The end of that speech hardly sounds like that of a victor, and Ramesses can hardly have been the only one who wished he were safe at home. However, all ends well, according to the poet; and in spite of the harsh things said to them the soldiers and captains finally praise their victorious king:

"Hail, splendid warrior, who encourages our hearts; you have saved your soldiers and your charioteers. Son of Amun, great warrior, you have destroyed the land of Hatti [the Hittites] with your strong arm. . . . All lands gathered together in one place have not withstood you; you won the victory before the army and in the face of the whole world. Here is no boasting. . . . You have broken the back of the Hatti for ever."

Here of course was most outrageous boasting, and the back of the Hatti was not broken for ever. Ramesses did in fact relieve the town of Tunip, thus erasing the shame of Amenophis III and Akhneten. But then he had had enough, and made a truce with his adversary and returned to his beloved Egypt.

There followed in due course a formal treaty of friendship between the two countries. The brother of Muwatallis was now on the Hittite throne, but Ramesses was still very much on the scene—his reign was most lengthy and he is supposed to have lived to the age of a hundred. We have knowledge of this treaty from both sources, Hittite and Egyptian, cuneiform as well as hieroglyph. It was an important document, after a very important battle. If the Hittites had won at Kadesh there might have happened what nearly happened after the widow queen's letter, a Hittite dynasty at Thebes. If Ramesses had won, the Egyptian Empire might have continued to flourish—which it did not. Perhaps the hysterical boasting of Ramesses II is a symptom of weakness: the Empire never really regained its full glory, and its decline, a slow decline, had begun.

The very fact that the Hittites had to be treated as a nation of equal importance shows the change that had come about. Egypt had to fear other enemies too, as in fact did the Hittites: somewhere in the background were "the People of the Sea" and more immediately the growing menace of a new people, a terrible people, the Assyrians. The treaty was in fact a defensive alliance. It ended thus:

And as for these words which are written upon these silver tablets for the Land of Hatti and the Land of Egypt: whosoever does not obey them, may the thousand gods of the Land of Hatti and the thousand gods of the Land of Egypt destroy his house, his land and his servants!

Bad luck on his servants! However, whether it was by the force of the combined two thousand gods or from a sound sense of reality, the treaty was in fact observed. And then, less than a century later, the Hittite capital had been invaded and burnt, and another ancient empire was rapidly fading into obscurity. . . .

As for Ramesses, he took to himself a Hittite princess as principal wife and lived on to his very ripe old age. Perhaps he was great; perhaps we have been a little unfair to him.

Old men forget; yet all shall be forgot,
But he'll remember with advantages
What feats he did that day.

In other words if Ramesses II had not lived so long he might not have harped upon Kadesh quite so much. There is one other thing which may make us sorry for him rather than impatient or annoyed. It is now believed that it was in *his* reign that Moses took his people out of Egypt.

Ramesses may have had the "spoiling" by the Jews and the Ten Plagues to contend with on top of all his other troubles.

Egyptian infantry: from a tomb model

14

END AND SUMMING UP

IT IS a little unfair at the least to dismiss the rest of Egypt's story in a few paragraphs. Yet Egypt is so long lived that by the time we reach the last thousand years before Christ we can rightly think of her ancient history and her own native greatness as over. By 1085 B.C. the third of the great periods, the New Empire, is finished, and the rest is largely decline and the suffering of invasion by foreigners. Do not forget, however, that there is something over seven hundred years to go before Alexander's conquest and the reigns of the Ptolemies, the era with which Champollion and the early decipherers were mostly concerned. These are the things that are impressive about the Egyptians: their ancientness, their unchangingness, and the long span of their greatness.

Before we try to sum them up, however, let us give these few paragraphs that will round off their ancient story.

Ramesses II was followed by no less than nine others of the same name. There being, it is said, no less than a hundred sons to dispute his succession, a period of confusion and usurpations after his death was not surprising. Then came the third Ramesses, perhaps really a greater general and monarch than Number Two. He beat the Libyans threatening from the west and the Aryan (or Aryan-led) "Peoples of the Sea", the latter fitly enough in one of the first recorded sea battles. He brought some prosperity back to Egypt. But he was *on the defensive*. After him, for the first time for over two thousand years, the Double Kingdom is no longer a united kingdom. Priests rule in a declining Thebes while separate kings rule in the Delta. This is the greatest time of tomb robbery, when that strange and desperate night removal of the sarcophagi took place. There must have been desperation, too, amongst the common people, for the terrors and increasing punishments of tomb robbery ever to have been faced.

Foreign dynasties now come to rule in Egypt, Libyans and dark Nubians from the south. There is some return of prosperity, even of grandeur—and at this time at the expense of the Jews. Solomon takes a Pharaoh's daughter as one of his wives. But soon after "Shisak, King of Egypt" has entered as a conqueror into Jerusalem. "And he took away," says the Bible, "the treasures of the house of the Lord, and the treasures of the King's house: he even took away all: and he took away all the shields of gold which

Solomon had made." The flow of gold has been reversed.

Not to much purpose, this booty, however. Civil wars return to Egypt; and repression; and revolts by the people against tyranny and crippling taxes, revolts that are brutally suppressed. Then comes real disaster from without: the Assyrians, whom Ramesses II had feared, at last appear at the gates. There is a respite, both for Egyptians and Jews, for the army of the dread Sennacherib is smitten by the plague—"And when they arose early in the morning, behold they were all dead corpses." Ashurbanipal meets no such misfortune, and in 666 B.C.—a nice round date for a terrible happening—he captures Egyptian Thebes. Yet the Assyrian occupation is short: fifty-odd years later and their capital Nineveh falls to the Medes and Persians. A short return of prosperity for Egypt and then the inevitable, for these are disturbed and terrible times: the conquerors of Assyria conquer Egypt.

That was in 525 B.C. In 332 Alexander conquers. In A.D. 30 the Romans. In A.D. 639 the Mohammedan Arabs. That is far enough to take the tale. Perhaps it was not so bloodstained and terrible in reality as it sounds in this concertina-squeezed account; most countries, our own included, have suffered repeated invasions and have survived. So has Egypt.

Now a summing-up.

First the character of the ancient Egyptian. He

was not cruel, that is to say by the standard of the times. Amenophis II in his ferocity was exceptional. By comparison with the Assyrians the Egyptians were cuddlesome saints. They were not naturally martial—even near the height of their Empire they seem, judging by the Kadesh poem, to have wished they were at home rather than campaigning in foreign parts.

They were intensely religious, yet often in so practical a way as hardly, as we would think, to be religious at all. All primitive peoples are rather like that: their "religion" is a mixture of super-stition and hard bargaining with the gods, almost a tussle with the gods to get the better of them and to get them on one's own side. The Egyptian in his religion is often extremely materialistic. Life on this earth was good; therefore build up your belongings, and bribe the gods, and muster all the magic formulæ; and you will carry on with an exactly similar, in fact even a rather pleasanter, life in the world to come! Spiritual subtleties, even much in the way of moral teach-ing, certainly anything in the way of metaphy-sical speculation, was foreign to them. They were not, one feels, very imaginative.

There was never for instance the gorgeous inventive fantasy and heroics of the myths and stories of the Greeks. The Egyptians had their stories, of course, and a few that were put to paper we have found. But they are not exactly thrilling. The favourite sort seems to have been a good sound moral tale, down to earth and with a happy ending. *Sinuhe* is one, told in the first person and with considerable complacency. It was the time of the Middle Kingdom; and at the death of the Pharaoh the conviction seems to have come to Sinuhe (he was a "Hereditary Prince and Count, Judge and District Overseer") that things would not go so well for him in the next reign. He therefore fled the country; and, after some wandering, fell in with an Amorite of Palestine, who (unlike the traitor Aziru) has a great admiration for Egyptians:

He set me at the head of his children. He married me to his eldest daughter. He let me choose for myself of his country. . . . It was a good land, named Yaa. Figs were in it, and grapes. It had more wine than water. . . . Moreover, great was that which accrued to me as a result of the love of me. He made me ruler of a tribe of the choicest of his country. Bread was made for me as daily fare, wine as daily provision, cooked meat and roast fowl. . . .

Sinuhe became the heroic ruler of his adopted tribe, and their saviour from the enemy:

I had let his weapons issue forth, I made his arrows pass by me uselessly, one close to another. He charged me, and I shot him, my arrow sticking in his neck.

That is the vulnerable point, where Achilles got Hector.

> *He cried out and fell on his nose. I felled him with my battle-axe and raised my cry of victory over his back.*

Even an unwarlike people likes to read of battle.

Then finally, in old age, Sinuhe is forgiven by the new Pharaoh for running away and is recalled:

> *"Do thou return to Egypt, that thou mayest see the home in which thou didst grow up. . . . It should not be that shouldest die in a foreign country. Asiatics should not escort thee"* (*i.e.* at his funeral).

So, still dressed as an "Asiatic" and in fear and trembling, he returns to the presence of his Pharaoh. He is lifted up, and given "a house which had a garden", a job, and the promise of a magnificent tomb which as was the custom is started before his death, his statue being "overlaid with gold"!

That is all. A "success story", in fact, and with the practical rewards of success not left to the imagination. It is relieved from grossness by at least a genuine love for home.

Nevertheless, though the Egyptian may have been an unimaginative, practical person, we must not forget or belittle his achievements.

His "practical" mastery of arithmetic and geometry and astronomy, for instance, was a very considerable achievement, and a promising one at that. Let us therefore shift our point of view a little and think in terms of achievement, and of what was the Egyptian legacy to the ancient world and so to our own.

There was a fashion fifty or so years ago to attribute everything to Egypt, to regard Egypt as the source and "cradle" of all civilization. That is not true. It must share the honours with the other river valleys. Nor is *everything* copied by one early civilization from another. Nevertheless the "land of the two kingdoms" does seem to have been the first genuinely united country, as opposed to a mere conglomeration of separate city-states. It was almost certainly the first to invent true writing, a sufficient claim to greatness. Later, other countries, Crete in particular, learnt from Egypt how to make things and make them beautifully, their crafts and their art. Egyptian paintings, making allowance for the disregard of perspective, one must recognize as at the least highly competent: powerful sometimes, and charming very often. Stop admiring only Greek statuary, and you may have time to admire Egyptian—as you should.

But the things of the spirit; ways of thought: what is the Egyptian contribution there?

The answer is: big; but not all good. The

Three works of art.   The cat is an amulet and has a gold
ear ring. The horse formed part of a whip stock. The duck
is an ivory ointment box

Egyptian, once more, had that handicap of being unspeculative. Not alone in this, he didn't like thinking. Even his language did not help him. Sir Alan Gardiner, the great philologist, who, you will remember, was among the first to enter Tutankhamen's tomb, says this: "The most striking feature of Egyptian in all its stages is its concrete realism, its preoccupation with exterior objects and occurrences. . . . Subtleties of thought such as are implied in 'might', 'should', 'can', 'hardly', as well as such abstractions as 'cause', 'motive', 'duty', belong to a later stage of linguistic development. . . ."

Perhaps that is the clue: in expecting something better we are expecting too much, Egyptian civilization being after all—and this is a pretty good understatement—somewhat early.

That is exactly what we must remember in considering the other very questionable legacy that the Egyptians handed on. Here they are not the only people guilty, but they are probably the worst culprits. We mean the legacy of *superstition*. There are no two ways about it: Egyptians were silly and muddled thinkers. Try to make logical sense of their intricate hierarchy of gods, and you will end in a lunatic asylum! Nor did they question things, the ways of Nature, the canons of behaviour, the riddles of the universe. All they did was to set up a Sphinx and not try to find out its secrets! They *accepted*. They believed as their forefathers had believed—which was a belief paramountly in portents and spells and incantations and spirits more often evil than benign, in other words in *magic*.

For the opposite of all this, for all that the Egyptians so signally lacked, we have to wait for the Greeks. *Theirs* is the enquiring mind, the healthily enquiring mind. Theirs in fact is the light, in contrast to the darkness of Egypt. . . .

This is perhaps no more than saying again that earlier the time was not ripe. We cannot expect the Egyptians to have been Greeks. More, the Egyptian phase was for mankind probably a necessity. Poor struggling *Homo sapiens* could not begin to be a Greek before he had been an Egyptian.

Nor must we forget Akhneten. The realism of his art, the beauty and sincerity of his poetry did not wholly die—not even wholly in Egypt itself, in spite of the ruthless counter-revolution. Perhaps the Jews, waiting for Moses, learnt something from the rebel king. Read the 104th Psalm, and see how it echoes the Hymn to the Sun, and not only echoes it but converts it into something more universal and more spiritual. So progress in the things that matter is made.

So, too, are we enabled to leave the Egyptians on an admiring note—which is as it should be.